Key Competencies for the Future

Key Competencies

for the Future

Rosemary Hipkins, Rachel Bolstad,
Sally Boyd, and Sue McDowall

NZCER PRESS

New Zealand Council for Educational Research
PO Box 3237
Wellington

© Rosemary Hipkins, Rachel Bolstad, Sally Boyd, Sue McDowall, 2014
All rights reserved

ISBN 978-1-927231-08-1
A catalogue record for this book is available from the
National Library of New Zealand

Designed by NZCER Press
Printed by About Print, Wellington

Distributed by NZCER PO Box 3237
Wellington New Zealand
www.nzcer.org
This title is also available as an e-book from www.nzcer.org.nz/nzcerpress

Cover photograph: Cameron Clayton, *Tolaga Bay at Sunrise.*
www.cameronclayton.com

Contents

Foreword, *by Alan Reid*	1
Introduction	4
Chapter 1	
Key competencies: The very idea!	8
Chapter 2	
Our futures-thinking process	19
Chapter 3	
Working with diverse others and ideas	32
Chapter 4	
Developing critical, self-managing, systems thinkers	51
Chapter 5	
Learning who to trust when knowledge claims conflict	72
Chapter 6	
Working together to make a difference	94
Chapter 7	
Key competencies for future-building educators	115
Chapter 8	
Our take-home messages	134
References	139
Index	143

Foreword

NEAR THE END OF the 20th century, as the economies and civil societies of all countries were being redrawn through forces such as globalisation and the technological revolution, educators began to speculate about the implications for how and what children and young people are taught in schools. Conferences were awash with talk of "education for new times", "skills for the 21st century", and the impact of these "changing times".

Given that the official curriculum is a formal representation of the knowledge that a society values, it is not surprising that from this ferment emerged many proposals for curriculum change. One of the key approaches was to identify many generic skills and understandings that are seen as being central to living in the 21st century, such as critical thinking, managing self, and relating to others. These were grouped under a catch-all heading—in my country, Australia, they are known as general capabilities; in New Zealand they are called key competencies—and placed alongside the disciplines or subjects in the official curriculum.

By the turn of the century, generic skills and understandings were a common feature of most official curricula. They promised to be an important strategy for making sure that students had the skills and understandings to live full and productive lives in the 21st century. Unfortunately, in my view, they have not delivered on that promise, mainly because of the lack of attention to their relationships to the learning areas, and the pedagogies through which they can be realised. That is, generic skills and understandings have been the least understood and the most underdeveloped aspect of the curriculum, and this has left them vulnerable. In Australia, for example, the general capabilities in the embryonic national curriculum have come under sustained attack. Most of the criticism stems from the lack of understanding about what they are, and the belief that they compete with, rather than enhance, the learning areas. If these criticisms are not met, the general capabilities will be abandoned by curriculum developers.

The work that is happening in New Zealand offers real hope that the potential of generic skills and understandings can be tapped. Over the past decade, the New Zealand Council for Educational Research (NZCER) has initiated many research projects and professional-development activities designed to engage New Zealand teachers with the key competencies. These programs have resulted in very positive learning outcomes as well as a rich repository of resources.

I have watched these developments in New Zealand with great interest, and I was thrilled to hear that many of the insights that have been generated from the work of a decade were to be distilled into this book. Now, having read the final version of the book, I can say that my optimism was well grounded. It has a number of important features.

First, the book is written in an open conversational style which invites the reader on an intellectual journey. It is an enjoyable read. Secondly, it locates the New Zealand key competencies inside a wider international framework by describing where the ideas came from and how and why they took particular shape. Thirdly, it explores the complexity of individual key competencies while demonstrating the importance of their interrelationship. Fourthly, it investigates the key competencies through a range of "wicked problems"—a clever heuristic by which to model pedagogies and to show how the key competencies are related. Finally, the book offers many well-thought-through and practical examples that show the exciting learning possibilities presented by key competencies.

The book is a wonderful vehicle for professional development, not only because of the key features I have described, but also because it does not preach or proselytise. Its authors spell out the values and assumptions which inform the choices made and the analyses conducted, but they do not provide answers. Rather they model the very processes they hope may take root in classrooms.

I congratulate Rose Hipkins and her team on producing a fine book which is going to be a very important educational resource, not only in New Zealand but in many other countries. It represents an important advance in the thinking about, and the practice of, key competencies.

Professor Emeritus Alan Reid AM
School of Education
Mawson Lakes Campus
University of South Australia
February 2014

Introduction

THIS BOOK WILL TAKE you (the reader) on a journey to explore engaging and relevant curriculum and schooling for students in this, the 21st century. We (the authors) began this journey with the shared assumption that we were digging into an important set of ideas that happen to go by the name "key competencies". For many teachers, the term itself won't need any introduction: New Zealand, like many other nations, had adopted a version of key competencies into the national curriculum. In this book, when we talk about the specific *New Zealand Curriculum* version, we refer to "*the* key competencies". We refer to the Organisation for Economic Co-operation and Development (OECD) version as "the OECD key competencies". And when we are more generally referring to ideas per se we simply talk about "competencies", or, as we'll soon explain, "capabilities".

We approach key competencies as metaphors to think with (rather than as more concrete things that students possess). This way of thinking about what key competencies really mean and what their presence in the curriculum is supposed to do could well be less familiar. In this book we move fluidly between two different sets of ideas. First, the idea of key competencies can be a stepping-off point for conversations about how students learn and the future of schooling. We use this type of idea about competencies to re-evaluate current practice and surface new possibilities for transforming the education system. The second set of ideas begins with each named key competency and dives deeper to explore their complex multifaceted natures. Neither way of thinking completely captures the essence of key competencies and the work they might do in the world. We didn't write this book to prescribe a "true" nature for key competencies, or to specify how anyone should work with them. Instead, our aim is to explore key competencies as a rich and complex set of ideas, and to sketch possible directions educators might take in their own work.

When the key competencies first arrived in New Zealand's school curriculum it was not obvious what schools should do with them. Schools we worked with were excited by the potential that the key competencies seemed to offer, and eager to explore their possibilities. Developing rubrics which identified core aspects of each competency was one common exploration strategy. Typically, these rubrics attempted to show what making progress in developing the competency might look like, using labels such as "emerging", "confident", and "expert". Later on, many schools became dissatisfied with their early rubrics and set them aside. But they didn't think creating the rubrics had been a waste of time. Instead, this process had helped them to unpack the complexity hidden in each key competency. They developed deeper and more nuanced insights into their natures as agents for curriculum change. We often heard these explorations described as steps on a journey of rethinking the school curriculum, rather than working towards clearly defined endpoints. Highly engaged teachers and school leaders recognised that developing a new vision is bound to create a few loose ends—living with some uncertainty comes with the territory.

Like our colleagues in schools, we are on the same journey. We too have found that a sideways move is sometimes necessary to then be able to move forwards. This book draws on and extends our learning journey towards a deeper understanding of the five key competencies that sit at the heart of *The New Zealand Curriculum* (*NZC*) (Ministry of Education, 2007). We are a small team of researchers from the New Zealand Council for Educational Research (NZCER). Together and individually we have worked with the key competencies since they were first considered for inclusion in *NZC*. Before the curriculum was published we did some preliminary work for the Ministry of Education. After the publication of *NZC* we investigated what was happening in schools that were quick to realise *NZC*'s potential for creating a vibrant, refocused, local curriculum that met their students' learning needs. Through a range of projects we have continued to research and write about evolving understandings of key competencies at the cutting edge of schools' work. These experiences are the foundation on which this book has been built—all the case study examples we use have come from New Zealand schools.

Why read this book?
Every time we've thought we had the idea of key competencies nailed we've found out there is more to learn! If you recognise this challenge, then this book is for you. We've written it for all the teachers and school leaders who are on a journey towards deeper understanding of the key competencies: their complex nature, how they could support real change in the curriculum that learners experience in school, and why making such changes really matters for our kids in their futures. We also hope to reach out to a wider audience—people who are interested in what's happening in education today, and why.

The history of ideas is important, especially when they are wide open to quite different interpretations. Knowing where ideas came from, and why, helps to determine an appropriate focus and framing for deliberations about them. So the first thing we do is to go back to the beginning, to look at where the idea of key competencies came from, and how we ended up with our very own New Zealand-specific version. We also briefly outline the different ways that people have been thinking about the key competencies so far, the limitations we can see—but also the potential for dynamic and forward-looking curriculum change. Next questions about the key competencies are the focus of the chapters that follow.

We've used a creative inquiry process, described in Chapter 2, to explore ways that key competencies could support real transformation in the school curriculum. If we really want to walk the talk of the fine-sounding 21st-century aspirations in *NZC* we can't just keep doing what we are already doing, but better. Our aim is to shine a light on possible, profound changes to the work of schools and the learning that students experience there. Throughout the book we draw on actual examples where inspired and inspiring teachers in a wide range of New Zealand schools are already showing the way.

1

Key competencies

The very idea!

LIKE ANY IMPORTANT IDEA, the concept of key competencies comes with its own history and baggage. We do know that much of what follows will be familiar territory to many of our readers who already work in schools. We promise to try to make revisiting the origins of the idea of key competencies worth your while. We also aim to reach out to readers who are less familiar with key competencies and other ideas about curriculum for the 21st century. If this is you, the following background might help you to understand how and why the school curriculum keeps on changing compared with the curriculum you experienced when you were at school.

The overall structure of *NZC*
NZC is what's called a *framework* curriculum. It isn't a prescribed list of things to be learned. Instead, the framework gives general signals about the sorts of learning students should experience and why those experiences were seen as important by the groups of educators who contributed to the development of the curriculum. Knowledge

isn't neglected—far from it. But instead of being set out in detail, the eight learning areas provide a high-level summary of important understandings and skills, and suggest where these might best belong in an overall learning programme. For those readers who are not familiar with its structure, Figure 1.1 shows the pieces of the framework called *NZC*. The most important idea to carry with you as you read on is that schools and teachers need to unpack and interpret these pieces for themselves. Ultimately, each school has the responsibility to design a curriculum that meets the learning needs of their students.

Origin of the idea of key competencies

In the middle of the 20th century, education policy makers in a wide range of nations had already begun talking about changes that might be needed for 21st-century education, and they tried to imagine what changes might be needed. Then in 1993 the United Nations Educational, Scientific and Cultural Organization (UNESCO) set up a groundbreaking project called the International Commission on Education for the Twenty-first Century. The project was led by Jacques Delors, a former chairman of the European Commission. By 1996 the powerful international team he led was ready to report back to UNESCO. Their report took the form of a book called *Learning: The Treasure Within*. This book is most commonly known these days as the "Delors Report".[1] In this report the many ideas about education for the 21st century that the commission had gathered were distilled down to four simple but powerful "pillars" of any education system. They said that every child was entitled to an education that would support them in:

- learning to be
- learning to know
- learning to do
- learning to live together.

These ideas opened up a space for many others to think more expansively both about the purposes for education, and about the sorts of outcomes

---

1. Links to this work, including the full report, can be found at http://www.unesco.org/delors/ (see Delors, 1996).

Directions for Learning

Vision
Young people who will be confident, connected, actively involved, lifelong learners.

Values
Excellence;
Innovation, inquiry, and curiosity;
Diversity;
Equity;
Community and participation;
Ecological sustainability;
Integrity;
Respect.

Key Competencies
Thinking;
Using language, symbols, and texts;
Managing self;
Relating to others;
Participating and contributing.

Learning Areas
English;
The arts;
Health and physical education;
Learning languages;
Mathematics and statistics;
Science;
Social sciences;
Technology.

Official languages

Achievement Objectives

Principles
High expectations, Treaty of Waitangi, Cultural diversity, Inclusion, Learning to learn, Community engagement, Coherence, Future focus

Figure 1.1: Detail from *NZC*, p. 7

of schooling that should be valued in education systems around the world. Learning to know and do were obviously already more familiar, but learning to "be" and learning to "live together" did—and still do—need a lot of unpacking and debate. For example, what might New Zealanders want our young people to "be" as a result of their education? This is a value-laden question, but *NZC* has attempted at least a high-level answer in the vision statement at the start of the curriculum document:

> Our vision is for young people:
> - who will be creative, energetic, and enterprising;
> - who will seize the opportunities offered by new knowledge and technologies to secure a sustainable social, cultural, economic, and environmental future for our country;
> - who will work to create an Aotearoa New Zealand in which Māori and Pākehā recognise each other as full Treaty partners, and in which all cultures are valued for the contributions they bring;
> - who, in their school years, will continue to develop the values, knowledge, and competencies that will enable them to live full and satisfying lives;
> - who will be confident, connected, actively involved, and lifelong learners. (*NZC*, p. 8)[2]

The Organisation for Economic Co-operation and Development (OECD) was one important group who further developed this expansive conversation on curriculum changes for the 21st century. From their work comes the idea of key competencies. The OECD runs the Programme for International Student Assessment (international tests that are commonly known as PISA). They use PISA assessments to compare the successes of different countries in educating their 15

---

2. We wanted to keep the text as uncluttered as possible so we decided that all direct quotes from *NZC* would be simply referenced with just the relevant page number. New Zealand teachers will be very familiar with this text already. Other readers can find a full version of *NZC* online at www.tki.org.nz. This website provides the official curriculum portal for materials generated on behalf of the New Zealand Ministry of Education.

year olds to be ready for the world of work and life beyond school. PISA results are used to demonstrate relationships between educational success and the economic prosperity of nations. Thus one of the OECD's overarching aims is to persuade governments to invest appropriately in the learning of all their young people.

The academic focus of PISA began with reading, mathematics, and science, along with problem solving. But PISA was created to test how well students can adapt and use their academic knowledge in contexts that are important for life and work. This aim meant that a traditional academic framework was not enough. The PISA programme needed to be informed by that certain something more which enables students to show what they know and can do with their learning. This challenge was too important for ad hoc question development. So the OECD established a large-scale consultation exercise to build a framework to guide the development of PISA assessments. That project was called DeSeCo (Definition and Selection of Competencies), and it culminated with the description of the OECD's version of key competencies.[3]

The DeSeCo project invited people from the various OECD nations to contribute their ideas about the things young people should be able to do to live a successful life in a well-functioning society. The specific question that guided the project was "what demands does today's society place on its citizens?"[4] The ideas that the DeSeCo researchers gathered were distilled to arrive at four key competencies. These four were identified as centrally important because:

- every student would need them, regardless of their life circumstances
- they were relevant across cultures and continents
- they were interdisciplinary—i.e. relevant to all learning areas of the curriculum.

Many other competencies had also been named, but these four were considered to be the foundation on which all the others could be built. Table 1.1 names these four key competencies and shows their main

---

3. A summary of the process can be found on the OECD website: www.pisa.oecd.org/dataoecd/47/61/35070367.pdf
4. This question comes from page 6 of the brief OECD report (see OECD, 2005).

Table 1.1: The four OECD key competencies

OECD key competency	What this competency entails
Acting autonomously	A. Act within the big picture B. Form and conduct life plans and personal projects C. Defend and assert rights, interests, limits, and needs *Acting autonomously requires individuals to develop a secure sense of their own identity, where they fit in, and an orientation towards the future that helps them think about where their potential might lie.*
Functioning in heterogenous groups	A. Relate well to others B. Co-operate, work in teams C. Manage and resolve conflicts *Students need to develop the ability to walk in others' shoes (i.e., empathy) which includes seeing issues from others' perspectives and thinking carefully about the dynamics of interactions.*
Using tools interactively	A. Use language, symbols, and texts interactively B. Use knowledge and information interactively C. Use technology interactively *Students need to understand how tools change the ways we can interact with the world. All types of learning tools are active meaning-makers, not just passive conveyers of ideas.*
Thinking	*Thinking reflectively was seen as lying at the heart of all the other key competencies. For this reason, thinking was described as a "cross-cutting" key competency.* *It's also interesting that this original DeSeCo version does not elaborate dimensions of thinking (i.e., A–C) in the same way as the other three were treated.*

Table 1.2: Comparing OECD and *NZC* key competencies

Name given to competency by OECD			NZC version
Thinking (cross-cutting)		Acting autonomously	*Managing self*
		Functioning in socially heterogenous groups	*Relating to others* *Participating and contributing*
		Using tools interactively	*Using language, symbols, and texts*
			Thinking (not identified as cross-cutting)

elements, as identified by the OECD. Beneath the OECD points A–C, we have added one idea about each competency, paraphrased from the brief DeSeCo report. Although these few words can only give a superficial reading of what the DeSeCo developers intended, we hope they serve to illustrate the hidden richness and subtleties of their intentions.

Did we lose something in translation?

Table 1.2 contrasts the OECD names with the names given to their *NZC* counterparts. Note that these are what we see as best matches, not one-to-one equivalents. *NZC* has five key competencies to the OECD's four.

What differences strike you as interesting? Well, first of all you may be wondering about why *NZC*'s developers positioned thinking differently. In *NZC*, thinking—as a key competency—has the same stand-alone status as the other four key competencies, whereas the OECD saw thinking as something that is integral to all demonstrations of competency. One reason the OECD gave for this is that reflective thinking is an important part of being competent. It's not enough to be able to just do something without being able to think about and critique one's choices and actions. This is an idea we will come back to again and again in the chapters of this book. Some respondents to the early drafts of *NZC*'s key competencies noted, however, that all the key competencies are used in combination. Thus the argument that *thinking* must be deployed alongside other key competencies can be applied to any mix of them (e.g., *managing self* is always being deployed in combination with the other key competencies). A second argument that surfaced during early consultation was that thinking itself is complex. It incorporates a wide variety of concepts and types of thinking. For this reason, positioning *thinking* as a separate key competency was seen as one way to get people talking about its scope, and hence develop shared understandings of what might be involved.[5]

Hindsight is a wonderful thing. After nearly a decade of working with the idea of key competencies it's possible to look back and see that the names developed for *NZC* do not necessarily convey the full richness of each competency, as intended by the OECD versions. What's immediately obvious if we compare Tables 1.1 and 1.2 is that the names the curriculum developers chose for New Zealand's curriculum cue subsets of each competency as devised by the OECD. For example, the bigger, richer picture could be lost if *managing self* is not seen as something done within the uncertainties of the bigger picture of any setting. Becoming autonomous is about so much more than demonstrating appropriate behaviour in a tightly managed learning context!

The DeSeCo idea that competencies are demonstrated in action was emphasised by adding a key competency called *participating and contributing* to the *NZC* set. In Table 1.2 we've aligned this key competency with "functioning in socially heterogenous groups" because

---

5. Justine Rutherford, a policy adviser in the New Zealand Ministry of Education at the time *NZC* was being developed, documented some of the important debates that took place. These were published in an article for the journal *Curriculum Matters*. Rutherford's paper highlights just how complex the very idea of key competencies was seen to be, right from the start of discussions in New Zealand (see Rutherford, 2005).

this is where action-based aspects of all the competencies might be most visibly and obviously demonstrated. The danger of this alignment is that "participation" might then be seen as only synonymous with group work in class. But consider, for example, the calibre of participation made by an individual who is functioning autonomously, compared with one who always needs to wait for direction. Key competencies are actually all cross-cutting of each other. We pull them apart to understand their individual character, but it's also important to stitch them back together when we put them to work in real contexts.

The idea of key competencies as capabilities
NZC describes key competencies as "*capabilities* for living and lifelong learning" (emphasis ours). It's right up there in the heading box on page 12 of *NZC*. Yet it has often been our experience that people can't immediately recall this definition when asked. We suspect it's easy to overlook! Indeed, the full implications of the idea of key competencies as capabilities have taken us some time to incubate ourselves. We now see this idea as pivotal to next questions about key competencies, and hence to the chapters that follow.

Combining "lifelong" and "capabilities" within an overarching definition of the key competencies carries some very big implications, especially when we consider that the key competencies are supposed to be woven through every learning area. How does today's subject-based learning (e.g., in English, or maths) provide opportunities for individuals to realise their potential as they live their lives, both now and in their future, however that unfolds? This question has important implications for how we think about the purposes for which students learn and the types of outcomes we should value. In turn, what we see as the important purposes for learning has big implications for what we should assess.[6]

---

6. That's a whole different can of worms. Assessment is not a main focus in this book because of space constraints—plus we think there are quite enough ideas to be going on with. Assessment challenges could well be the focus of a whole book in their own right. Once new directions for learning have been debated and agreed, assessment matters are the logical next focus for curriculum conversations.

If learning is to connect meaningfully to students' lives, as *NZC* says it should, the bigger purpose that the teacher has in mind will need to be deliberately developed. The learning will almost certainly encompass something more than traditional content acquisition for its own sake. With the OECD's ideas about reflective development of competencies in mind, we can also predict that this expansive purpose will need to be made evident to students, so that they know why they are being asked to do whatever it is that is the action focus of the learning. Our comments here address "why" questions, but there is still the important matter of "what" to consider.

What will today's students need to be capable of doing and being in their lives beyond school? We can begin to address this question by unpacking the multifaceted intent of key competencies, as set out in Table 1.1. Doing this could help us arrive at rich sets of capabilities, defined as specific things the learner might do now, or aspire to do next. What worries us, though, is that this type of curriculum thinking can be constrained by what is already familiar. It has been our experience that some teachers respond to any suggestions of competency-related curriculum changes by saying "we already do that". They are not being cynical—these teachers really don't see that something more than today's best practice might be required. This type of response most probably reflects a failure to appreciate that how we understand what a curriculum *is* has shifted in recent years. As we've seen, key competencies are essentially a curriculum idea—they are not specific things. They can't be treated like a prescription that has been set out for people to decode and then just follow (like, say, a traditional list of curriculum content to be learned). Key competencies require careful interpretation by everyone who uses them. Because communities, schools, teachers, and students are so diverse, this dynamic process of interpreting needs to happen as close as possible to the teaching and learning action. This is the essence of building a local curriculum. The payoff is likely to be learning that engages and empowers everyone involved, but we certainly won't be claiming that it's easy to achieve.

Working together, school leaders, teachers, and learners need to be supported to keep on engaging with the idea of competencies and capabilities, creatively generating deeper and richer insights and learning experiences as they go. We've learned a lot from our work with teachers and school leaders who are already doing this, and they have learned from the new idea spaces we have helped open up. Ongoing collaboration as everyone learns together is the name of the game.

Future-focused thinking is one important area where we see that we can contribute some fresh ideas. Today's students are almost certainly going to face some challenges that today's adults did not encounter when growing up in different times. Is it possible to imagine sets of capabilities that bring with them an element of future-focused learning? This is the agenda we have set ourselves for the chapters that follow, beginning with an outline in Chapter 2 of the futures-thinking process we used. We would like to model a process that others can also pick up and use for their own curriculum thinking.

2

Our futures-thinking process

The title of our book, *Key Competencies for the Future*, contains two very big ideas—"key competencies" and "the future". While many of us know quite a lot about the key competencies (in theory at least), the big, challenging, more impossible-to-know questions hang squarely over the future end of our thinking. In this book, we focus on bringing the future, with all its unknowns and uncertainties, into the foreground. In doing so, we open a challenge for ourselves: to use ideas about the future to build backwards to ideas about the development and expression of key competencies by learners and teachers in the present.

Building on some of our other work,[1] we adopted the idea of using "wicked problems" as a means of thinking ourselves forward into futures that we can't yet see clearly. This chapter outlines why we saw wicked problems as a generative framing for our futures thinking, and what we did to develop the thinking behind this book. But first, we hope to convince you that *NZC* conveys some important messages about what a future-focused curriculum should look like.

---

1. In 2012 we worked with Jane Gilbert on a discussion document for the New Zealand Ministry of Education about future-oriented learning. This paper introduced the idea that students needed to learn in ways that could help them cope in a word beset by wicked problems (see Bolstad et al., 2012).

How NZC positions key competencies within a future focus

The eight principles in *NZC* are described as the "foundations of curriculum decision making" (p. 9). One of these is the *future focus* principle:

> The curriculum encourages all students to look to the future by exploring such significant future-focused issues as sustainability, citizenship, enterprise, and globalisation. (p. 9)

On a skinny reading, this principle could be seen as a signal to include topics about the future somewhere within the overall curriculum. But we think it is important to make a more expansive framing of what this principle means. A fatter reading of this principle could begin by asking what it might mean for students to look to the future (and, by implication, to their own futures). This becomes a very potent question to address if we then add the intention for the principles to act as foundations of decision-making across the whole curriculum. How is today's learning, in whatever learning area, helping young people look to their personal futures—to be and become the people they are capable of being?

We've already seen in Chapter 1 that *NZC* describes the key competencies as "*capabilities* for living and lifelong learning" (our emphasis). Putting the lifelong idea in that definition sends clear signals that learning is not just about being capable now, but being capable of continuing to learn across one's whole life span. In this way, both the principles and the key competencies point to the importance of thinking about our young people in their futures when building a local curriculum. *NZC*'s vision sets out an idealistic account of "what we want for our young people" (p. 8). Who wouldn't want them to be the "confident, connected, actively involved, lifelong learners" described in the vision? These attributes are such self-evidently good things that it would be hard to find dissenters. But what does all this rhetoric actually mean where the rubber hits the road—that is, in the classroom, during day-to-day teaching and learning? That's a much trickier question, but again there are some useful and interesting signals at the overview level of the curriculum.[2] Here are just two—you'll be able to find many more:

> As they learn a language, students develop their understanding of the power of language. They discover new ways of learning, new ways of knowing, *and more about their own capabilities*. Learning a language provides students with the cognitive tools and strategies to learn further languages and to increase their understanding of their own language(s) and culture(s). (p. 24, our emphasis)

> In science, students explore how both the natural physical world and science itself work so that they can participate as critical, informed, and responsible citizens in a society in which science plays a significant role. (p. 17)

Both of these are direct quotes from the overview section of *NZC* which outlines the contribution each of the eight learning areas makes to a "broad, general education" (p. 16). The first quote is from the expanded version of the statement about the contribution that the learning area called Learning Languages makes to the overall curriculum. There is a definite future focus to the argument being made. The contribution of this learning area is much more expansive than simply being able to speak another language when relevant. Capability here is seen to have important dimensions related to self-awareness and, yet again, learning today as preparing for future learning. The second quote is the more pithy one-sentence version that defends science's place in the curriculum. Notice that what's signalled arguably still lies mostly in the future. Students learn science now so that they can become capable adult citizens when confronted with decisions in which some science

---

2. See Figure 1.1—by the "overview level" we mean the vision, principles, values, key competencies, advice on effective pedagogy, and the two-page "essence statements" that describe the contribution each learning area makes to *NZC*. These pieces are sometimes referred to as the "front half" of *NZC*. The things that they signal are supposed to be woven together with the more traditionally specified "content" of each of the eight learning areas, which collectively make up the "back half" of *NZC*.

knowledge will help them make an informed choice. (Notice also that this argument says nothing about what sort of knowledge that should be—this is a question we will come back to later in this book).

All in all then, putting key competencies—defined as capabilities—at the very heart of the curriculum provides a fresh way of asking future-focused questions about what today's students will need to be capable of in their lives beyond school. But no-one can know what lies in their future with any certainty. Life is capricious, and none of us can tell exactly what might happen to us. To some extent, life's contingencies (relationship successes and challenges, work-related ups and downs, small accidents and so forth) are able to be predicted from our own and others' experiences. Much more difficult to address is the complex and self-reinforcing mix of social, technological, and environmental change that is taking place very rapidly, globally as well as locally. Everyone faces an unknown future in which experience is not necessarily a reliable guide to future learning and coping needs.[3] That's why we developed our own process for trying to think differently about what being capable might mean in a future-focused framing. We started with the idea of wicked problems.

What are wicked problems?
While there is much to celebrate about humanity's achievements and accomplishments, you may—like us—be worried about the many signs that all is not well in the world. There are ongoing serious challenges and some new ones that are growing increasingly difficult to ignore: climate change, depletion of fossil fuels, environmental degradation, biodiversity loss, economic crises, poverty, food security, and lack of access to equitable educational opportunities, to name just a few. Today's students will face new sets of problems in their futures, as all

---

3. When Ronald Barnett addressed the question of what might be involved in *Learning for an Unknown Future* he used a thought experiment. What, he asked, are the attributes of people who know what to do when no-one knows what to do? His list of dispositions (p. 258) is helpful (carefulness, thoughtfulness, humility, criticality, receptiveness, resilience, courage, and stillness) but this still begs the question of what and how day-to-day learning contributes to their development (see Barnett, 2004).

problems are of their times, and some gain prominence before receding. These very different issues have quite a few things in common. All span multiple domains: social, economic, political, environmental, legal, and moral. Each of them interacts with, or is embedded within, other related problems. None of them present a clear set of alternative solutions—different solutions can create or exacerbate other problems. All involve "contradictory certitudes"—that is, different people or groups believe they "know" what the answer is, but these answers are irreconcilable with one another. For these reasons, all are "highly complex, uncertain, and value-laden".[4] Because of these characteristics, some theorists have begun to call them "wicked problems".[5]

It is difficult to find simple, optimal solutions for wicked problems—not because they can't be solved, but because it is extremely difficult to reach agreement about what should be done. Importantly, the wickedness of these problems means that they cannot be solved using straightforward puzzle-solving, or solutions from only one knowledge domain or paradigm. Theorists have suggested that wicked problems can be addressed by bringing together disparate perspectives on the problem. If different people see the problem from a range of perspectives, then all these viewpoints need to be brought to the table. In doing so, people can begin to search for "clumsy solutions". As the name suggests, it is almost certain that these solutions will be imperfect (because of the wickedness of the problem), but at least clumsy solutions might provide steps in a useful direction. Beginning with a clumsy solution can also open up space for further solutions to emerge, mitigating new problems that will inevitably arise when this initial solution is applied.

Pause for a minute and think about the educational implications of the 21st-century challenges and realities of living in a world beset with wicked problems. What obvious mismatches can you see between the very idea of wicked problems and the way the school curriculum

---

4. See Frame and Brown (2008, p. 226). We are grateful to our colleague Bob Frame from Manaaki Whenua/Landcare Research for introducing us to the notion of wicked problems and pointing us in the direction of a rich and interesting literature on this topic.
5. See Rayner (2006) who attributes the identification of wicked problems to Horst Rittel, a professor of Planning at the University of California, Berkeley, in the late 1960s.

has traditionally been organised, taught, and assessed? And where are the opportunities to develop key competencies in all this? These are questions we will come back to again and again in this book.

Wicked problems as a useful conceptual tool for educators
It should already be obvious that we think 21st-century education ought to support learners actively to develop the capabilities they need to engage productively with wicked problems and their possible clumsy solutions. While these problems are difficult and challenging, they are the undeniable fabric of life in today's world. Addressing them is a big challenge for most of us who have been educated in a system that was successful in supporting many kinds of learning, but rarely put complex problems at the very centre of educational attention. Nor did the education most of us experienced focus specifically on developing capabilities needed to engage productively with open-ended 21st-century challenges. Taking this idea seriously means having to carefully rethink the ways that educational planning and design are approached. Teachers and other education leaders also need to recognise that even experienced educators may not yet have the kinds of expertise needed to support learners to become capable of engaging with wicked problems. However, we are optimistic that we—and you—*do* have the capacity to develop this expertise. Taking on our own challenge, we decided to tackle some wicked problems ourselves, and think through their educational implications.

Our process for futures thinking was as follows. Each of us chose a wicked problem, and we tried to spread these across a wide spectrum of human concerns. We then followed the same series of steps, beginning with choosing from the media one or more stories that discussed at least one aspect of our chosen problem. We then analysed our stories to identify:
- the nature of the problem (as presented in each story)
- the nature of the solution proposed or implied
- the ways in which people were seen to be contributing to the problem

- the ways in which people might contribute to the solution
- the ideological perspective
- any gaps or silences—that is, aspects of the problem that had not been raised or addressed by any one story.

Once this initial work had been done, we drew on our own knowledge of key competencies to identify aspects of capability that the analysis seemed to raise. Here, we asked ourselves three questions.

- What would students need to be capable of being and doing, in order to cope in a situation where this wicked problem became pressing for them or others?
- What would the capabilities we identify mean for their learning right now?
- What might the capabilities we identify mean for supporting students to get ready for life beyond school?

The point of working backwards was to try and get at deeper layers of each *NZC* key competency that might be overlooked within a more traditional framing of the key competencies and learning areas.

After each of us had tried the process out individually, we came back together to pool our thinking. Everyone presented their problem and their view of its implications for key competencies. We then critically discussed the conclusions we had reached, drawing out similarities and differences and debating the nature of the various capabilities that seemed to emerge across our analyses. In this way, we refined the collective thinking on which the following chapters are based.

On our soapbox

Every worthwhile book has an agenda, whether that's obvious or not. With this in mind, we felt it was important to try and be transparent about our own values and how they have influenced our framing of the discussion of the key competencies in the chapters that follow. So here in Box 2.1, just briefly, is one thing each of us really cares about, followed by several more general points we wanted to make explicit.

Sue

What does it mean to teach for diversity?

When I was a teacher I thought I knew the answer to this question, and I thought that I was pretty good at it. I began my career in a multilevel classroom in a small rural school that also included a few "townies" like me. Back then, I thought that teaching for diversity meant that all my students—regardless of their age, ethnicity, first language, culture, religion, social class, living arrangements, strengths, and needs—would see themselves represented in my classroom, and know that they belonged. I selected from the National Library service books for silent reading in which my children's interests and experiences were represented. I did morning greetings in different languages. We sang waiata and learnt te reo Māori. We did open-ended art and writing projects with space for diverse and creative responses. We did co-operative learning in mixed-ability groups. I also went to some lengths to expose my students to diverse others beyond the classroom. We had pen pals from a school in another, quite different part of New Zealand. We made friends with people in the local old people's home, and visited what was then called the disabilities centre. I still think these were good things to do. But now I can see that we hardly ever used the diverse ideas of our class and community for real purposes. The activities I set up made space for diversity; they did not require diversity to do the work. What interests me now are activities or problems that rely on diverse ideas—activities or problems that are more fun, more challenging, more achievable, more successful, and more satisfying when diverse ideas must be drawn on. We look at how this might happen in Chapter 3.

Rose

Do we really believe the whole can be more than the sum of the parts?

We hear this saying quite often, but when I think back over my years in teaching, and now in education research, I see many bits that never quite got connected up to create dynamic wholes. I taught my subjects in pieces (science and biology) because that's the way secondary school systems are organised. More recently, I've worked on my various research projects without necessarily having the

Box 2.1: On our soapbox

time to look across them. The constraints of the ways we organise our work and learning are very real, and it sometimes seems like making changes is just too hard. But that's exactly what complex systems thinking challenges us to do. That's where the idea that the sum can be more than the parts comes from, and it's a big field of scholarship that's changed the whole way I see the world. When I began to explore complex systems thinking some implications hit me really hard. I realised how much we assume that the future will be much like the present or the recent past. I've read enough now to be convinced that complex systems really can turn on a dime. They absorb pressures until suddenly they can't take any more and everything changes. It scares me to think how hard we are pushing our earth systems right now. I'm really interested in how we can get more of our kids to be good systems thinkers, without scaring them into the feeling that whatever they do is futile anyway. That's a fine balance, and it's been a constant point of reference for us as we've worked on this book. You'll see these ideas threaded through Chapters 4 and 5 in particular.

Sally
Learning at school needs to support students to engage in authentic actions that make a difference to their world.
It's common to read statements like this these days but so what? "Authentic" is an overused word so we need to be clear what we mean. When we say "authentic actions" we mean opportunities to do real-life tasks or in-depth projects about issues students really care about, but which are also important to the wider community. These projects usually involve students working as a team or with people outside school. You'll see examples throughout this book. We've seen in our own research, across many projects now, how passionate students and teachers can be about doing something for real. Carefully co-constructed authentic actions can be highly motivating for students. We all know that engagement is a key enabler of current learning, but we've also got young people's futures in mind. These experiences provide rich opportunities to develop the key competencies, and they help students to see themselves as people who

Box 2.1 (*continued*)

have agency in the world. Authentic learning can have its messy moments that take us all out of our comfort zones. Hearing how teachers and students have worked through the dilemmas they face made me realise I needed to shift my views about young people and learning. I now know that young people have the ability to make the world a better place: they're not citizens in waiting, they're citizens now! Why should they have to learn about how other people make a difference before they can do so themselves? This question challenges all of us because we often hear from students that these opportunities are not always available in their classrooms. In this book we've tried to walk the talk: every topic we've chosen is one where students can take agency, and we've tried to show what that might look like at different stages of schooling. Chapter 6 specifically explores how students can work collectively to make a difference to their world.

Rachel

We must all take on the challenge of being futures thinkers.

I've spent the last few years wrestling with the question of what it really means to take a future-oriented approach to education. I have also applied this question to myself: What do I need to do to become a better futures thinker and more future-oriented educational researcher?[1] I have realised one thing: being a futures thinker is actually quite hard, and taking a future-oriented approach to education is no easy matter—for anyone. However, I believe it can also be extremely liberating to take on thinking challenges that seem just a bit too hard. Diving deep into futures thinking has certainly had this effect for me. So are you willing to step up to face the unknown and ask questions that you can't know the answers to yet? Are you excited by the idea of fishing out something previously tossed into the too-hard basket and starting there? If you answered yes to either of these questions then you are well on the road to being a futures thinker, and this book is most certainly for you. You will hear more from me in Chapter 7.

---

1. Rachel has blogged about these kinds of questions on Shifting Thinking (www.shiftingthinking.org). See also Bolstad (2011), http://www.nzcer.org.nz/research/publications/taking-future-focus-education-what-does-it-mean

Box 2.1 (*continued*)

Taking a future focus

While the soapbox is still out we'd like to say just a little more. The intellectual ground on which we stand is composed of shared commitments, assumptions, and values. From this shared ground we look to the future. We realise that not everyone will agree with all that we have to say—we sometimes disagree with one another. But in the spirit of walking our talk, here are several ideas about the future of education that have influenced the ways in which we have built our shared understandings of what key competencies are and what curriculum work they should do.

Educators are often told that education must be future focused and adaptable to meet changing learning demands for an increasingly complex world. However, we know this is much easier to say than do—for many reasons. As with many kinds of change, it is often easier for all of us to see what we are moving *away* from (for example, the gradual shift away from a one-size-fits-all approach), than to imagine exactly what it is we are moving *towards*. People frequently talk about "21st-century learning" when talking about the need for change, but we don't think this can be pinned down to an exact formula or a simple set of strategies. Future-oriented learning isn't out there waiting to be discovered and put into practice. We see it is an emerging cluster of new ideas, beliefs, knowledge, theories, and practices that, understood together, can help point us in the right direction. *NZC* and *Te Marautanga o Aotearoa* are flexible and enabling frameworks, and the vision, values, and principles provide a strong foundation for teachers and school leaders to take a future-oriented approach.[6] But they alone are not enough.

Work that we and our colleagues have done suggests at least two big ideas need to form a core part of our future-oriented educational thinking. The first is to shift how we view knowledge, and the second is the need to redesign educational approaches so that they are based on

---

6. For more on this see: http://nzcurriculum.tki.org.nz/content/download/21774/214653/file/NZC_Update_26_ONLINE.pdf

what we now know about learning.[7] You can read more about how these ideas apply to *NZC* elsewhere;[8] our point is that they challenge many of the assumptions which underpin current educational practices, as well as some assumptions which many people in the community hold about education. If we are seeking to transform education, many more of us will need to get our heads around these new ideas about knowledge and about learning. This practical need means the ideas themselves can't be too abstract, jargon-laden, or theoretical; they can't just bounce around pages of academic journals or get talked about in education conferences. They need to make sense to kids, parents, teachers, and many other people. They need to connect with what people already believe is important about learning, as well as stretching the collective imagination about the future of learning. The ideas need to connect with actions we can all take in our own spheres of influence, at home, at school, in the community, in our professional work. We agree with Charles Leadbeater (2011, p. 6) that:

> a new consensus needs to be forged about the kind of learning we should aspire to provide, a consensus that parents, children and teachers can buy into in the everyday life of going to school as much as policymakers designing the education systems of the future.

This book is our contribution to the challenging agenda of building a consensus about what a future-focused curriculum might look like. We see the key competencies as a useful vehicle for driving this agenda forward. Our research has shown that the key competencies have been well received in schools, but we can see how the intent of the changes they signal could easily be overwhelmed by other changes that have come along later. With this book, we hope to return the key competencies to centre stage, explore their deeper layers, and consider how we might use

---

7. The ideas we introduce very briefly here are developed much more fully in Jane Gilbert's book *Catching the Knowledge Wave?* (Gilbert, 2005).
8. See: http://nzcurriculum.tki.org.nz/content/download/21774/214653/file/NZC_Update_26_ONLINE.pdf

them to make *NZC* really sing. What might a new vision for curriculum look like? We have in mind a curriculum that really does put the learners themselves at the heart of their learning now. Learners would also keep in sight the important knowledge and skills they must learn, while holding a clear view of where the outcomes of that learning might support them to venture in their futures.

Looking ahead
Each of the following chapters follows a similar, but not identical format. Each begins by briefly introducing one of the wicked problems that we explored and goes on to address the capabilities within each key competency that we saw as fitting most tightly with that problem. In every chapter we draw on a range of examples from the cutting-edge practice of some of our teacher collaborators. You'll find primary- and secondary-school examples threaded through the chapters. We invite you to think about how you might adapt the many capabilities that contribute to each key competency, and the learning actions we use to illustrate their development, so that the ideas can work a range of curriculum levels.

As we sequenced the chapters and confirmed what to elaborate where, we were forced to confront the challenges posed by the linearity of text. The various capabilities we discuss apply across most or all the wicked problems, but space in the book prevents us constantly circling back. Perhaps you would have chosen a different sequence to ours—or chosen to pull out different points in certain contexts. We hope so, because that would mean you are doing the same sort of futures thinking as we have challenged ourselves with.

3
Working with diverse others and ideas

Being Kiwi: Diversity all part of life

ARE NEW ZEALANDERS
REALLY ALL PART OF
ONE BIG HAPPY FAMILY?

MIND YOUR LANGUAGES
Cultural diversity is something to embrace

Figure 3.1: News media headlines

Our global world

How does the mix of students in today's classroom compare with the classes of your own school years? It's not hard to see how local communities are becoming more diverse. As well as the increased diversity resulting from physical mobility, all of us are also learning to cope with a sort of virtual mobility. Rapid advances in information and communication technologies are increasing many people's access to diverse others around the world. More than ever before, each one of us is likely to be living alongside or working with people from social, cultural, and linguistic backgrounds that differ from our own.

Globalisation is a contributor to many wicked problems. Learning to live with increased diversity and its consequences is just one example.[1] But the diversity that comes with globalisation also provides the possibility of working towards clumsy solutions to these other types of problems. Addressing wicked problems involves bringing together different perspectives and ideas. It's important to remember that this bringing together involves more than ensuring the presence of a range of values, knowledge, and expertise. It involves more than respecting and more than understanding this range. Working towards possible solutions to wicked problems involves drawing on diverse sets of values, knowledge, and expertise, and using them in new combinations or ways.

Working with diverse others and ideas to solve complex world problems is difficult because (as described in Chapters 5 and 6) it is value laden, it usually requires those involved to adapt or radically change their world views, and it involves some groups giving up conditions which have historically been to their advantage. These are not things any of us do naturally or easily. People will not necessarily develop the capabilities for doing them without learning how and having opportunities to practice and develop them.

---

1. Increasing income disparities, which are the stepping off point for Chapter 6, are also at least partly caused by the impact of globalisation on financial systems of different nations. This note serves to illustrate the point that we've made a choice of "angle" to take when thinking about the implications of the different wicked problems introduced in the different chapters.

Capabilities needed for working with diverse others and ideas

It is easy to see why working with diverse others and ideas is important. What is not so clear is what this work involves and how to practise it. This work requires the capacity to learn new ways of being in the world, or what James Gee calls "discourses". He describes discourses as the ways particular groups of people (for example, certain sorts of lawyers, women, families, cultural groups, and so forth) behave, interact, value, think, believe, speak, read, and write: "Discourses are ways of being 'people like us.' They are 'ways of being in the world'; they are 'forms of life'; they are socially situated identities."[2]

According to Gee, students are already proficient in many discourses on arrival at school. These discourses include the primary discourse of their family and community groups, and secondary discourses such as their understanding of how to be a gymnast, a Catholic, a collector of rugby cards, or a bike owner. At school there are new discourses to learn, including those related to being the member of a classroom, school clubs and teams, and those related to different subject areas, such as science, mathematics, and English.

The key competency *using language, symbols, and texts* is described in *NZC* as "working with and making meaning of the codes in which knowledge is expressed" and as recognising how the use of these codes "affect people's understanding" (p. 12). This description resonates with Gee's ideas about discourses. In the 2006 draft curriculum document,[3] the following statement was included in the description of *using language, symbols, and texts*, but in the final version of *NZC* it is found in the learning areas section:

> Each learning area has its own language or languages. As students discover how to use them, they find they are able to think in different

---

2. This quote comes from *Sociolinguistics and Literacies: Ideology in Discourses* (3rd edition) (Gee, 2007, p. 3). In this book, James Gee describes a theory of how language functions in society, along with techniques for the study of language and literacy in different contexts.
3. The draft version of *NZC* was published in 2006 and then revised in response to extensive feedback. Much of this feedback can still be viewed in the archives section of the *NZC* website: http://nzcurriculum.tki.org.nz/Archives

ways, access new areas of knowledge, and see their world from new perspectives. (p. 16)

It seems a pity that this statement did not remain in the description of *using language, symbols, and texts*. Without its inclusion, it becomes too easy to interpret this competency simply as the literacy and numeracy competency—that is, business as usual. So, to sum up the argument, students need to be able to talk each other's talk (and not talk past one another) to become capable in conversation with diverse others.

Although we foreground the importance of *using language, symbols, and texts*, the other competencies are also important for working with diverse others and ideas. Many of the ideas associated with *using language, symbols, and texts* can also be found in the key competency *thinking*. *NZC* describes *thinking* as the capacity to "actively seek, use, and create knowledge" and to "draw on personal knowledge and intuitions, ask questions, and challenge the basis of assumptions and perceptions" (p. 13).

Different discourses, such as those associated with different learning areas, involve not just languages and texts but also identities and practices[4]—that is, the different ways in which people see themselves and behave. These ideas are referred to in *NZC* descriptions of the key

---

4. Being part of a discourse community requires people to "take on" or enact particular *identities*. James Gee (2007) argues that: "People cannot learn in a deep way within a semiotic domain if they are not willing to commit themselves fully to the learning in terms of time, effort, and active engagement. Such a commitment requires that they are willing to see themselves in terms of a new identity, that is, to see themselves as the kind of person who can learn, use, and value the new semiotic domain" (p. 54). Moje (2008) talks about the need to engage in "literate practice" in disciplines or subject areas. According to Moje, the focus needs to move "away from accessing or generating texts only to obtain or produce information toward an understanding of how texts represent both the knowledge and the ways of knowing, doing, and behaving in different discourse communities" (p. 103). Draper and Seibert (2010) describe disciplinary literacy as "the ability to negotiate (e.g., read, view, listen, taste, smell, critique) and create (e.g., write, produce, sing, act, speak) texts in discipline-appropriate ways or in ways that other members of the discipline (e.g., mathematicians, historians, artists) would recognise as "correct" or "viable" (p. 30). And according to Shanahan and Shanahan (2012), "disciplinary literacy emphasizes the unique tools that the experts in a discipline use to engage in the work of that discipline" (p. 8). These conceptions of literacy involve much more than the capacity to read and write—they involve the capacity to "do" the discipline, i.e., to learn and use the discourses of a discipline.

competencies *managing self, participating and contributing*, and *relating to others*.[5]

The capacity to work with diverse others to solve complex problems also requires social and emotional skills, such as the capacity for empathy—to stand in the shoes of others. Students need to know how to listen and engage with others, and to express alternative viewpoints respectfully. *NZC* describes students who manage themselves as "enterprising, resourceful, reliable, and resilient". In the draft version of *NZC, managing self* is also described in terms of identities: "It is about students knowing who they are, where they come from, and where they fit in." (p. 11)

While the statement above is not included in the final curriculum document, traces of these ideas remain and are important to remember in the context of working with diverse others and ideas. For example, *NZC* says that *relating to others* is about:

> interacting effectively with a diverse range of people in a variety of contexts ... the ability to listen actively, recognise different points of view, negotiate, and share ideas. Students who relate well to others ... are aware of how their words and actions affect others ... by working effectively together, they can come up with new approaches, ideas, and ways of thinking. (p. 12)

Being aware of how your "words and actions affect others" is also a component of knowing and managing yourself. Interestingly, the words above were originally included in the description of *managing self* in the 2006 draft curriculum. They were shifted into the description of *relating to others* as the final version of *NZC* was prepared. This switch signals how closely linked these two competencies are.

---

5. *NZC* describes *managing self* as students "seeing themselves as capable learners" who have "strategies for meeting challenges"; *participating and contributing* as "the capacity to contribute appropriately as a group member"; and *relating to others* as being "able to take different roles in different situations" (p. 12).

Teaching for the capacity to work with diversity
The education system has not traditionally provided students with many opportunities to engage with diverse others and ideas. Students tend to be grouped with others of the same age and "ability". And although students move through the education system in groups, and have opportunities to work with others, most assessments still focus on individual rather than collective learning.

Nor has the education system traditionally provided students with many opportunities to bring together diverse sets of ideas. The curriculum is divided into separate learning areas and students are expected to specialise if they wish to become experts in particular disciplines. School students have traditionally had few opportunities to build new knowledge. This has been the domain of the university, by which time students are considered to have "acquired" the "foundation" knowledge and ways of doing things associated with their discipline.

Limitations on students' opportunities to learn are due, in part, to assumptions about the mind, knowledge, and learning underpinning the current education system. These include assumptions that:

- knowledge is true, stable, discipline-specific stuff that is developed slowly over time by experts, and that is located and can be passed between the minds of individuals
- minds are like containers which store and process knowledge
- learning (the process of storing knowledge in individual minds) occurs at roughly the same rate for students of the same age.

These assumptions persist, even though they are not consistent with what we now know about the human mind and about learning, and even though they are not consistent with the ways in which knowledge is currently thought about and used.[6]

Future-oriented scholars have been arguing for some time now that one of the ways we can help students build the capacity to work with

---

6. Jane Gilbert (2005) describes these types of assumptions as mental models which become so part of our everyday thinking that we forget to think about them as models and begin to treat them as common sense. For an accessible discussion of the assumptions, or mental models, about minds, knowledge, and learning that underpin the evolution of the education system, see pages 68–75 of *Catching the Knowledge Wave?* (Gilbert, 2005).

diverse others and ideas is by focusing on what goes on in the spaces between ideas and between people rather than on the ideas or on the people themselves.[7] Some New Zealand teachers are working within the constraints of the current system to provide their students with opportunities to do this. In Box 3.1 we have included examples from some of these teachers' classrooms.

Example 1

To what extent is Cinderella's father to blame for her predicament?

This first story comes from *Life Long Literacy*[1]—a project focusing the integration of key competencies into classroom reading programmes in the middle primary school.

A Years 2 and 3 teacher involved in the *Life Long Literacy* project wanted her students to shift from seeing reading as uncovering the author's meaning to having agency and authority as readers. She wanted them to make meaning in the way that literary critics do—by using evidence from the text, and their knowledge and experiences. The teacher aimed to do this by creating a classroom reading environment similar to that of a book group and by modelling the ways in which literary critics engage with text, and with the interpretations

---

1. *Life Long Literacy* (Twist & McDowall, 2010) reports on a project in which a group of researchers supported eight teachers of reading in the middle years of the primary school to conceptualise the key competencies more deeply and to design and implement reading programmes which integrated the competencies. The report can be found at:
http://www.nzcer.org.nz/research/publications/lifelong-literacy-integration-key-competencies-and-reading

---

Box 3.1: Opportunities for building the capacity to work with diverse others and ideas

---

7. In the article "Education for the Knowledge Age: Design Centred Models of Teaching and Instruction" (Bereiter & Scardamalia, 2006), Carl Bereiter and Marlene Scardamalia talk about the need to view knowledge advancement as a community, rather than individual, achievement. In the book *Catching the Knowledge Wave?* (Gilbert, 2005), Jane Gilbert talks of the need to provide opportunities for working in the spaces between people. In the book *Engaging Minds: Changing Teaching in Complex Times* (Davis, Sumara, & Luce-Kapler, 2008), Brett Davis, Denis Sumara, and Rebecca Luce-Kapler argue for a knowledge-centred curriculum in which there are opportunities for diverse ideas to bump up against each other, rather than a teacher- or child-centred curriculum.

of others. She used the text, *Cinderella: An Art Deco Love Story*[2] and posed this question: "How much is Cinderella's father to blame for her situation?" She got her students to analyse the character of the father—his appearance, dialogue, actions, and thoughts, and what the author tells the reader about him. Initially, most students held strongly onto the concept of the ideal father and drew on it heavily when thinking about how responsible Cinderella's father was. However, as students became more skilled at analysing the text and illustrations, and at using these as sources of evidence, a wider range of views emerged.

The teacher observed that, while students had learnt relatively quickly how to defend and challenge interpretations, it took some time for them to learn how to adapt or change interpretations in response to those of others. Some students found it especially difficult to tolerate the uncertainty that comes with loosening the grasp on one interpretation in order to take hold of another. One student in particular got very upset when another challenged his interpretation of the father's character. The other students working in a group with these two came running to the teacher in alarm, saying "There's a fight." Her interpretation of the situation was that it was "a really good conversation" in which the students concerned had not quite mastered the self-management skills needed to debate ideas. She saw the disagreement and the response of others in the group as evidence of the need for more practice in hearing and responding to alternative interpretations.

Example 2

Should Waitangi Day be kept as our national holiday?

This story comes from a recently completed research and development project called *Key Competencies and Effective Pedagogy*[3]—a project focusing on the integration of key competencies and learning areas.

---

2. The authors of this book are Roberts and Roberts (2001).
3. The *Key Competencies and Effective Pedagogy* project explored the integration of key competencies into learning areas in the primary and secondary school. The materials developed from this project can be found at: http://keycompetencies.tki.org.nz/Key-competencies-and-effective-pedagogy

Box 3.1 (*continued*)

A social studies class of Year 9 students used a range of sources to investigate different viewpoints on the question "Should Waitangi Day be kept as our national holiday?" and created a for-and-against graphic. Students then chose one side of the issue and inquired further into the arguments that supported this specific perspective. The class then held a carefully structured discussion of the question. The teacher based the structure of the discussion on the Philosophical Chairs model.[4] In this model, students with opposing views on an issue sit facing each other across the centre of the room. Students who do not have a position sit in the neutral zone, at the bottom of the U formation.

The general rules were written on the board: "Think before you speak—organise your thoughts; Address the ideas, not the person; Listen when others are speaking—don't interrupt; Move if your view changes based on the arguments you hear; After you speak, wait until two others on your side have spoken." As well as these general rules, students were given a rubric highlighting the features of positive and negative contributions to a discussion.

The discussion started with large numbers supporting the retention of Waitangi Day as a national holiday. Only a couple of students were opposed, and about six were neutral. As the discussion progressed, interesting comments and questions were made by students in all three areas, and some people started physically moving their chairs between the different positions in the discussion.

Example 3

How should New Zealanders' involvement in war be memorialised?

Our third story comes from a Year 10 social studies teacher, who wanted his students to understand that the National War Memorial is a deeply contested space and, in developing this understanding, learn how to think like historians. The unit started with theme finding: everyone shared and analysed personal or family memories of Anzac Day. One theme that emerged was that the stories shared were almost entirely about soldiers. Did other people have experiences

---

4. Philosophical Chairs is just one discussion model. More information on this and other discussion models can be found at www.lawanddemocracy.org/discussionmodels.html

Box 3.1 (*continued*)

of war too? Students also discussed a photograph of an elderly man wrestling with a much younger hippie on Anzac Day in the 1970s and being separated by a policeman. Other stories of Anzac Day controversy and opposing viewpoints on what this day means were discussed and debated among the class. The teacher then raised the concern that the memorial does not recognise New Zealand's "foundational wars of colonisation" and told a brief story of the invasion of the Waikato in the 1860s.

Students then spent several weeks considering two central historical questions: "Why did New Zealand men go to war in 1914?" And, "Why did New Zealanders object so strongly to conscientious objectors?" Both questions required students to interpret evidence as they took historical perspectives to build their argument. Students were then given an inquiry task where they could choose any war New Zealand has been involved in and investigate the nature of this involvement.

The final part of the unit shifted from explicit historical reasoning to moral reasoning. Students had to respond to the question: "How should New Zealanders' involvement in war be memorialised?" by designing a memorial space for the empty zone across the road from the National War Memorial awaiting development by the Ministry for Culture and Heritage. They had to work as a committee of citizens debating what their memorial should look like. To support their thinking, students were provided with a framework that outlined five key approaches to the memorialisation of war. The final designs, a mixture of physical models, Google SketchUps, and architectural style drawings, were displayed for parents and teachers.

Example 4

How can we sustain the Uawanui?

The final story comes from a project that was possible because of a web of relationships which had developed over a number of years between Tolaga Bay Area School, the University of Otago, Te Aitanga-a-Hauiti, the Uawa Tolaga Bay community, the Allan Wilson Centre, and many other people and organisations in the local community and the science community.[5]

One ongoing project that stems from these relationships aims to ensure economic, environmental, cultural, and social sustainability across the Uawa River catchment. At one stage of this project, a group of Years 11–13 students participated in a 3-day marae-based science wānanga. This involved students, teachers, tangata whenua, and a team of scientists and postgraduate science students from Otago University and the Allan Wilson Centre working together on a shared long-term project—restoring the Uawanui river mouth. The science wānanga was one in a series with the purpose of raising the engagement and achievement of rangatahi in science. The kaupapa, or agenda, of the science wānanga series is to provide students with hands-on science opportunities in their local community using a collaborative approach that values mātauranga Māori and science in building a socially, economically, and environmentally sustainable future.

The wānanga began with a pōwhiri held on the first afternoon, giving time for the students, teachers, scientists, and other manuhiri to be welcomed and meet one another. Activities then covered zoology, botany, forestry, and cultural mapping. They included: observing impacts from forestry, farming, and residential housing along the river; developing pictures of the area and the important parts of it for the community; measuring stream health through macroinvertebrate and fish identification; comparing plant transect surveys at restored and unmaintained riverbank sites; and collecting and preparing herbarium samples to be maintained at the school where mātauranga Māori and

---

5. The background to the science wānanga is discussed in *Strengthening Engagements between Schools and the Science Community* (Bolstad et al., 2013). The report can be accessed at http://www.nzcer.org.nz/research/publications/strengthening-engagements-between-schools-and-science-community. The Uawa River restoration project is also described here: http://www.groundtruth.co.nz/content/sustainable-future-tolaga-bay-uawa and in a 2012 article in the *New Zealand Education Gazette*, "Acknowledging History for Future Planning": http://www.edgazette.govt.nz/Articles/Article.aspx?ArticleId=8634

Box 3.1 (*continued*)

other science knowledge pertaining to each species could be stored and shared. The students were involved in identifying ways of achieving environmental and community sustainability across the area.

Establishing a marae-based approach meant that students had access to the science knowledge which the University of Otago could provide. The University of Otago science partners also had access to the cultural knowledge which the community was willing to share. An important aspect of the project was the willingness of the science partners to take on board the ideas and aspirations of the community, and open and honest relationships in which partners could ask for help or collaborate to develop projects together. Student observations suggest that both the scientists' and the community's ways of thinking and working had changed to better solve shared problems, such as how to sustain the Uawanui:

> All the people that come on the wānanga, not only do they give their knowledge freely, but they absorb the way that *we* think, they consider it ...

> We're already bringing science into the community, but mixing it with our culture. The way we do things on the marae, the way we do things and the way we live, it's just really cool to mix those up [with science learning].

> It seems like they are making science fit the community, not the community has to fit into science ... It's not just science, but for me going onto the marae all the time, it's given me new insight into everything as a person. Talking to random people, it's how some people just have one view of things, [whereas] now you have a whole different perspective of science, Māori, European, everything.

Box 3.1 (*continued*)

Back to the capabilities
In this section we describe how, by foregrounding the key competencies, teachers provided students with opportunities to build their capabilities for working with diverse others and ideas.

Using language, symbols, and texts and *thinking*
In all cases in Box 3.1, the teachers provided students with opportunities to learn the languages and ways of *thinking* associated with particular learning areas. The history teacher, for example, provided his students with five key approaches to the memorialisation of war to consider when making their own decisions about how war should be memorialised in New Zealand. He provided his students with opportunities to use the language of historians as they read, discussed, and wrote about memorials, photographs, historical documents, frameworks, and commentaries; and to use the language of citizens as they worked to determine how New Zealand's involvement in war could best be memorialised. The primary school reading teacher modelled—and provided her students with opportunities to use—the language of literary criticism to analyse the print text and illustrations of a picture book.

In some of the examples in Box 3.1 there were opportunities to bring together the languages and ways of *thinking* associated with different disciplines or world views to solve shared problems. The science wānanga, for example, provided students and scientists with opportunities to draw together ways of thinking from Western science and mātauranga Māori, and to think across social, economic, and environmental factors. The scientists had opportunities to learn the languages and ways of *thinking* associated with mātauranga Māori, with pōwhiri, and with other aspects of wānanga participation. Likewise, the students and other members of the local community had opportunities to learn and use the languages and ways of *thinking* associated with Western science, such as learning the languages associated with species classification, with relationships between plants and animals, and with different forms of mapping. As a result, new ways of using language and ways of *thinking* began to emerge.

Participating and contributing, relating to others, and *managing self*
Teachers in the stories did not just give their students opportunities to learn the languages and ways of *thinking* associated with different disciplines. The teachers also provided students with opportunities to learn the ways of *managing self, relating to others*, and *participating and contributing* associated with these disciplines.

The primary school reading teacher, for example, modelled what a "real" reader looks like. She took part in informed discussions with her students, modified her interpretations in response to the interpretations of others, and modelled using a literary text to make sense of herself, others, and the world.

Across these stories there are fewer examples of opportunities for students to compare the ways of *managing self, relating to others*, and *participating and contributing* associated with different learning areas or domains or to experiment with and adapt these. However the student quotes at the end of the Uawanui story suggest that the students involved in this project were beginning to do so. There was some evidence to suggest that, as a result of the collaboration, new ways of doing science and of being in the world emerged to solve a shared problem—sustaining the Uawanui.

So far we have been talking about the *NZC* key competencies as they play out when associated with different disciplines or domains. There are also more personal and emotional components to the key competencies required to work successfully with diverse others and ideas. These include the capacity to listen to, and take on board, different viewpoints, and to disagree or suggest alternative approaches in constructive ways.

Some teachers provided students with structures to help them explore diverse viewpoints. In the Treaty of Waitangi story the teacher supported students to express and respond to alternative perspectives in a safe and productive way. The Philosophical Chairs model provides three things. First, the model creates a safe space (the neutral zone) for students who are not initially sure of their viewpoint or who do not initially have the confidence to express it. Secondly, it gives students who do take a position the choice of whether to share publicly the reasons for that position. Finally, it provides opportunities to change one's mind without losing face. The rules also contributed to the safety of the environment, and at the same time served to make explicit the nature of both positive and negative contributions to a discussion (something it is often assumed that students know).

The primary school reading teacher provided her students with two quite different opportunities for building the capacity for empathy. One was the opportunity for students to relate to the characters in the picture book they were reading and to understand the relationships between those characters. The other was for students to relate to their peers and their range of interpretations which were based on differing experiences. Both opportunities were safe—the first, because the world of Cinderella is a fictional one, and the second, because the students were working in a guided and supported context in which disagreements were encouraged, rather than frowned on. The response of the students to the fight demonstrates how little opportunity the students involved had experienced in their prior years of schooling to express and discuss alternative perspectives and to deal with disagreement.

The Uawanui story shows the most overt opportunities for building the capacity to relate to others by setting aside time for the sole purpose of relationship building. The very first step in the project involved providing time for tikanga processes and whanaungatanga, for the students, teachers, scientists, and other manuhiri to be welcomed and meet one another. It was only after establishing relationships that collaborative work on the shared problem of sustaining the Uawanui began.

The place of knowledge

It is important not to overlook the place of knowledge in the four stories. In a recent article on disciplinary literacy, Elizabeth Moje explores the conundrum of how to help students to learn the languages, practices, and identities associated with a discipline if they do not have the necessary background disciplinary knowledge. Moje also considers how students can build disciplinary knowledge if they have not acquired the languages, practices, and identities associated with the discipline.[8] The teachers referred to in this chapter all engaged in practices consistent with the conclusion Moje comes to. That is, they made sure that students had access to the established disciplinary knowledge with which to think, talk about, relate to one another, and reflect on their own values, beliefs, and perspectives. The primary school teacher provided her students with the Cinderella text and with information about how fictional characters are constructed. The social studies and history teachers both provided their students with opportunities to do their own research to help them develop individual and group perspectives on their topics of inquiry. In the project *Sustaining the Uawanui* the marae partners provided the scientists and students with access to local people with mātauranga Māori related to sustaining the Uawanui, the team coordinating the wānanga provided tikanga support for manuhiri, and the scientists shared knowledge from Western science.

It is important to note that the teachers did not insist that students investigate existing knowledge before engaging with diverse others and ideas to solve problems. Rather, they set up opportunities to explore existing knowledge alongside opportunities to build new knowledge, feeding in access to existing disciplinary knowledge if, when, and as students needed it.

Opportunities to learn

Across these stories there is a progression in the complexity of the problems students were working on. The Years 2 and 3 students in the Cinderella example worked on building a shared understanding of an ambiguous character in a picture book, while the students in the Uawanui project explored a web of interrelationships that contributed to the sustainability of a river and local area.

There was also a progression in the degree of diversity (of people and ideas) with which students had opportunities to engage. The Years 2 and 3 students engaged with the diverse perspectives of their peers, the

---

8. See Moje (2008), "Foregrounding the Disciplines in Secondary Literacy Teaching and Learning: A Call for Change".

characters in a picture book, and with the perspectives of the author. In the Uawanui project, students engaged with a range of ideas (from mātauranga Māori and Western science) and people (students from other schools and of different class levels, and community members including marae elders, scientists, members of the forestry industry, landowners, and people who live near waterways).

Despite these differences, all students had opportunities to use group diversity to build knowledge that was new, at least to their group, and that was useful to the group for further knowledge advancement.[9]

Next steps

So how do educators go about providing students with the opportunities they need for building the capabilities to work with diverse others and ideas? From the four stories presented in this chapter, and other stories from practice we have come across in our work as teachers and researchers, it seems there are eight important things to do.

1. ***Set up a task with space for a variety of viewpoints***. In all stories, teachers provided their students with something to think about by posing questions for which there was no one right or wrong answer, such as: To what extent was Cinderella's father to blame for her predicament? How should war be memorialised in New Zealand? Should we keep Waitangi Day as a national holiday? How can we best sustain the Uawanui, socially, environmentally, and economically?

2. ***Help students access the existing established knowledge as and when it is needed to help solve their shared problem***. The history teacher, for example, told his students about the invasion of Waikato in the 1860s; and the primary school reading teacher taught her students about text features.

3. ***Support students to build knowledge and capabilities***. The capacity to work with diverse others and ideas requires students not just to know how to think, use language, participate and

---

9. See Bereiter (2002), who describes knowledge building as the process of creating conceptual artefacts that can be used for further knowledge building.

contribute, relate to others, and manage oneself in different ways—it requires the capacity to actually do these things in an integrated way and in real situations. With this in mind, it is important to note that teachers did not just provide their students with explicit instruction or practice exercises to help them to develop each capability. They provided them with opportunities to use these capabilities through *participating and contributing*, *relating to others*, and managing themselves in apprentice or real discourse communities.

4. ***Provide opportunities for students to work with others***. In all cases, teachers provided their students with opportunities to work with others. The history students, for example, were required to work as a group to decide how war in New Zealand should be memorialised.
5. ***Ensure group diversity***. Think about students' age, skills, knowledge, interests, ethnicities, gender, first language, social class, living arrangements.
6. ***Provide opportunities for diverse ideas to emerge and collide***. Simply having a pool of diverse ideas is not enough. There need to be opportunities for the collision of diverse ideas. The teachers in all these stories enabled such opportunities.
7. ***Provide opportunities for collective knowledge building***. Often, there were opportunities for group or collective (rather than just individual) ideas to emerge.
8. ***Provide opportunities to revisit ideas over time***. In many cases, the teachers provided the students with opportunities to think critically about, question, and alter, adapt, or improve on ideas that were on the table. The children studying the Cinderella text, for example, were taught how to use evidence from the print text and illustrations, along with their knowledge and experiences, to question, refine, or alter group interpretations of the father's character. In all cases, teachers provided students with opportunities

to change their mind if they had reason to do so. Sometimes this opportunity was structured into the learning activity. as in the use of the Philosophical Chairs model used by the social studies teacher.

It's time to move on. We began this chapter with globalisation, which can be seen as a contributor to multiple wicked problems. Then we explored the ways in which the increasing cultural and linguistic diversity that comes with globalisation makes it possible to work towards solutions for wicked problems when we are able to bring diverse sets of knowledge and values together in productive ways. In the next chapter we move on to look at the question of food security—a much more concrete and place-based wicked problem—and we explore opportunities for students to develop systems thinking.

4

Developing critical, self-managing, systems thinkers

Fat people threaten global food security

FED UP WITH HUNGER
Catholic Church focuses on food security

OVERFISHING JEOPARDIZES GLOBAL FOOD SECURITY

Figure 4.1: News media headlines

Food for thought

HUNGER IS A WICKED problem—anyone paying attention must know there are hungry people all over the world. There are, of course, degrees of hunger, from extreme starvation in war-torn or drought-ridden places, to the less-visible hunger of urban poor people everywhere, including in New Zealand. Many of us have contributed to efforts to alleviate this suffering of others. What is less visible to most of us is our role as part of the problem. To understand our involvement we need to begin with some brief explanations about the concept of food security and why it is a wicked problem. Once the scope of the issue has been addressed, we'll be better placed to consider the sorts of capabilities that could help our young people to respond appropriately to the challenges that arise when people lack food security.

Here are two definitions of food security, each made by a New Zealand organisation that is working to address this problem. Notice how both convey the same basic message, but the second one goes further by drawing attention to behaviours that might, in effect, conceal the issue from wider public scrutiny:

> The ability to legitimately and regularly access safe and nutritionally adequate food. (Caritas)[1]

> Access to nutritionally adequate, safe and personally acceptable foods without being anxious about how and where to acquire it or resorting to makeshift coping strategies such as begging, scavenging, or relying on emergency assistance such as food banks. (Christchurch City's health profile statement)[2]

We happened to complete our analysis of news articles during a social-justice month in New Zealand in 2012. In this one month there were

---
1. The full press release can be found at: http://www.scoop.co.nz/stories/PO1209/S00075/fed-up-with-hunger-catholic-church-focuses-on-food-security.htm
2. Read the full discussion at http://www.healthychristchurch.org.nz/city-health-profile/the-profile/factors-that-affect-our-health-and-wellbeing/toiora/food-security.aspx

many stories related to food security in the news media, including two of the three headlined stories in Figure 4.1. At the time of writing this chapter, in mid-2013, food security was again a hot topic in the news, although this time it was seldom given that name. The specific aspect being hotly debated was whether hungry children should be fed at school if their parents do not, or cannot, feed them adequately at home. Several cartoonists contributed to the public controversy with visual references to parents taking advantage of government generosity for their own selfish purposes. Shortly, we will consider how one secondary teacher used such material for teaching purposes.

The snapshots of three different dilemmas in Box 4.1 are based on the articles we collected during the social-justice month in 2012, or on the food-in-schools controversy that erupted a year later. These snapshots illustrate why wicked problems are called "wicked". Notice that what is seen as the problem by some can be seen as the solution by others. Also, if one challenge is solved, others could well be inadvertently caused as a result.

Something else that's really interesting is that only a handful of the articles we collected in 2012 focused on how all of us are part of the problem. For all the different dimensions that were covered in the articles collected, this one critical aspect remained relatively invisible. "Fat people threaten global food security" was one article we found that came close to positioning people who are not going hungry as part of the problem, but unfairly laid the blame with one group who are (perhaps rather smugly) "not us" if we are not overweight. So what's missing here?

When we buy cheap food, we need to think critically about why it is cheap. A bumper crop in a great growing season is one thing. But it is a quite different matter if the growers and gatherers of unreasonably cheap food are not being adequately recompensed, or the land on which the food is grown is likely to be unsustainably degraded, or a combination of both. When we buy cheap food produced in these types of circumstances, we unwittingly contribute to food security problems elsewhere.[3] When meat is very cheap, it's possible that the animals from which it is produced have suffered. In other countries, sheep and cattle suffer when they are raised under intensive housing conditions, and in these conditions they are likely to have been subjected to treatments that could ultimately harm people (for example, though overuse of antibiotics). While such intensive beef and sheep farming does not happen in New Zealand, pigs and chickens can be raised intensively, and these do tend to be our cheaper meat products.[4] The point is, our personal choices are not neutral and they are not just our own business. Sometimes they're not even really choices, because the food concerned is the only food of that type people can get. Even so, our food choices do have real consequences elsewhere that are not immediately apparent to us.

These comments about personal choices (especially unwitting ones) need to be counterbalanced by drawing attention to the wider systems, politics, and associated regulations that drive food production and distribution locally, nationally, and internationally. Many choices are beyond our direct control as individuals, local groups, or even sovereign nations. Unless educators help our young people understand how personal action and choices are unavoidably embedded within dynamic, sometimes global, systems with all their associated politics, they will not be adequately prepared for their future roles as citizens of New Zealand and stewards of planet Earth. That is why the main focus of this chapter is the development of students' capabilities for systems thinking.

‿

---

3. A book that addresses this issue for a range of specific foods is *Not on the Label: What Really goes into the Food on your Plate*, by UK journalist Felicity Lawrence (see Lawrence, 2004).
4. An illuminating discussion of this issue can be found in Michael Pollan's book *The Omnivore's Dilemma* (Pollan, 2006). For a vivid fictionalised account, Ruth Ozeki's book *My Year of Meats* is worth a read (Ozeki, 1998).

Dilemma 1
Food in schools: Whose responsibility?
Over the last decade food prices have increased at a faster rate than average incomes, and food security in New Zealand has declined sharply. Drawing on the Adult Nutrition Survey conducted in 2008/2009, one research project found that only 35 percent of Māori and 26 percent of Pasifika people were fully, or almost fully, food secure, compared with 64 percent of New Zealand European and other participants.[1] Very few people would dispute the reality that many children go to school hungry, and that Māori and Pasifika children are over-represented among hungry or poorly nourished kids because more of them come from low-income families. What is often hotly disputed is what should be done about it. Some people think it should be the parents' responsibility, and that even if it is a struggle, they should be able to find money for nutritious food. Some of this group see irresponsible parents as the problem (e.g., because they spend their money on other priorities). People who advocate for children to be fed at school argue that hungry kids should be fed so that they can learn. Their parents' situation is not their fault. Many in this group see poverty as the causal problem, not parental irresponsibility. From a wider-system perspective, those who oppose food in schools would say that the government has no business to be feeding children, and it will just make their parents even more irresponsible, or dependent on handouts, or both. Some who support food in schools would counter by arguing that nourished children will be healthier, learn better, and be less likely to be a drain on government funding as they get older. Many people take a middle position somewhere between these two arguments.

Dilemma 2
Ecological impacts of food production
Many people in poorer nations rely on wild fish for protein, or income, or both. If their fishing activities were to be forbidden these people would starve or

---

1. This is from the Master's thesis research of Hayley Stevenson, University of Otago, retrieved from http://otago.ourarchive.ac.nz/handle/10523/2274

Box 4.1: Three food security dilemmas

be severely malnourished. However, local fish stocks are not being managed sustainably and are in decline, so some people think a ban should be enforced. (When the fish are gone, the people will starve anyway.) The World Wildlife Fund (WWF) advocates a different solution. If poor fishers could be supported to develop a holistic suite of ecosystem- and science-based measures to manage their fisheries sustainably, local subsistence economies would do better. For the WWF, the real problem is large-scale fisheries operations that flout quota regulations and exploit workers in poorer countries (not usually the countries where the fishing conglomerates are based). The burden of trying to stop these activities tends to fall on the poor nations where they happen—and they can't afford the necessary countermeasures. WWF says what is needed to solve this problem is international co-operation to control illegal and unregulated fishing. From another perspective, demand for moderately priced fish products in wealthier nations (e.g., tinned tuna or omega oil products) makes these very large operations as profitable as they are. Some commentators on global food security would say that we in affluent nations need to pay a more realistic price for such food. But this, of course, would compound the challenges for poorer New Zealanders, as outlined in Dilemma 1.

Dilemma 3

Trapped in a food desert

Inadequate nutrition can be a relatively invisible aspect of poor food security in an affluent society. People don't necessarily have to go hungry to lack food security, and effects of continual malnourishment can have lifelong health and learning repercussions for children. One real challenge here is that fast food is often oversupplied in poor communities. Supermarkets or other types of food retailers are not usually located in poorer communities. Areas where fast food is the only type of food on offer are called food deserts.[2]

---

2. Carly Woodham, another researcher from Otago, has suggested that our lower socio-economic areas might be better thought of as food swamps: there is plenty of food, but it is not healthy food. http://otago.ourarchive.ac.nz/handle/10523/1655

Box 4.1 *(continued)*

> It can be harder for people living in food deserts to buy fresh food if they cannot afford private transport to get to the retail outlets that sell other types of food. In any case fast food quickly alleviates hunger because it tends to be high in fat, is served in large portions, and is available very quickly on demand. But it is cheap for a reason and is not a healthy choice when it is eaten regularly. So living in a food desert perpetuates and sustains the poor nutrition aspect of food security problems.

Box 4.1 (*continued*)

The three dilemmas in Box 4.1 illustrate the contested and controversial nature of wicked problems such as food security. Historically, the school curriculum has avoided these sorts of issues in favour of more settled knowledge that almost everyone can agree about.[5] Our goal in this book—and we hope your goal too—is to find ways to be more proactive and deliberate in the ways we educate our young people for their futures. One clear implication is that we can no longer afford to sidestep these sorts of topics because they don't feel so safe for teachers. So how do we find new ways forward? As we now explain, we see the development of systems thinking as one proactive way we can manage the unavoidable tensions of making deep changes in the nature of the curriculum we teach.

Systems thinking as a specific dimension of *thinking*

This chapter foregrounds systems thinking as just one of many dimensions to the overall key competency *thinking*. On one level, systems thinking is easy to understand. We could simply picture it as joined-up thinking that happens when learners establish connections between ideas and events, where those connections might otherwise remain hidden from their experience. The links between ecology and economics developed in Dilemma 2 (Box 4.1) are a good example of

---

5. This argument is developed in Michael Apple's classic book *Ideology and Curriculum*. While the writing context is American, the points he makes apply widely across nations with a history of publicly funded education for young people (Apple, 2004).

this sort of connecting across knowledge areas and experiences. While it is easy enough to describe joining-up of this nature, making connections across subject-based curriculum divisions isn't necessarily easy to do.

Practising systems thinking ourselves challenges all of us to consider the impact of different contingencies. Systems in the physical world are dynamic and often unpredictable. One event can determine what comes next and trigger a whole cascade of changes. A different initial event or set of conditions might trigger a different set of changes in the same system. As we've seen in Chapter 3, social systems also behave in contingent ways. A specific way of understanding a context might trigger certain ways of responding that would not be chosen by someone who had a different understanding about what was happening, and why. We could view this type of contingent thinking as "it depends" thinking. The example that follows illustrates this "it depends" thinking in a simple assessment task.

"It depends" thinking
NZCER's science education team coined the term *"it depends" thinking* when analysing an Assessment Resource Bank (ARB) item.[6] Years 9–10 students had been asked to respond to a hypothetical change in a simple food web describing feeding interactions in a home garden. Figure 4.2 shows what the students were given.

One question asked students to say what would happen to three other animals if a gardener used a spray that killed all the aphids and whitefly. Most students described definite effects, for example, "The spiders will die of starvation". The researchers were coding these responses as correct or incorrect according to the links in the food web when they came upon a small number of answers such as this one:

> Spider—won't have the aphids or whiteflies to eat so will either die or prey heavily on wasps. Wasps—will either have no spiders eating them

---

6. The item and the teachers' notes can be accessed on the ARB website: http://arb.nzcer.org.nz/resources/science/living/2000/lw2000.htm. The item is called "A Garden Food Web" and its number is LW2000. Note that you need a password before you can access the ARBs.

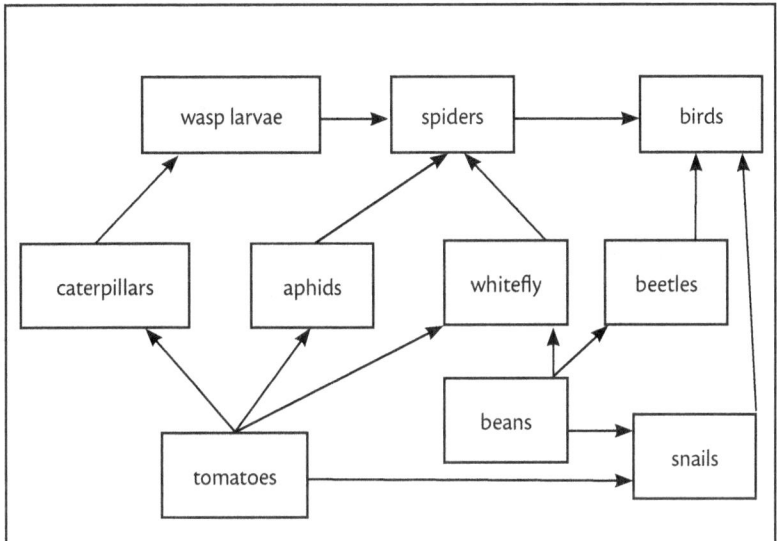

Figure 4.2: A typical simple food web

(because they died from lack of aphids/whiteflies) or will be eaten a lot more.

This type of response really challenged the researchers to think again about the judgements they were making. The students who responded like this were all from the same school. They showed a more nuanced and dynamic understanding of how food webs work than the majority of students who gave simple right/wrong responses. "It depends" thinking describes these nuanced responses. The researchers recoded all the other responses to see if students in other schools might have demonstrated the same awareness of how systems work. No other students had shown this perceptiveness—but how could they have done so, if they were unaware of this possibility? How often does a simple right-or-wrong judgement of answers to assessment questions serve to conceal and discourage more insightful critical thinking about how the world actually works?

Complex systems thinking adds yet another dynamic to *thinking* as a key competency. Complex systems adapt to absorb change, and they can absorb a lot of it without seeming to be affected. When change does eventually occur in complex systems, it is non-linear and not fully predictable. It is said to be emergent. For example, you can push your body really hard, or neglect a minor health issue, and for a time nothing seems to happen. Then quite suddenly what seemed minor can become a major crisis. This happens because the parts of complex systems interact with each other and they don't necessarily do just one job, or respond the same way in all circumstances.[7]

Complex systems are embedded within, and interact with, other complex systems, again with emergent results. (For example, individual body cells are tiny complex systems, each of which contributes to the overall activities of an organ, then an organ system, then the whole complex system we call our body.) It should be evident, even from this very brief introduction, that helping students to understand and practise systems thinking has a number of layers of complexity.

If we take the challenge of educating students for this century seriously, we must develop their systems-thinking capabilities—with all the demands this implies. The next section of the chapter explores the mix of capabilities that need to come along for the ride when we're following the call of systems thinking.

How all the key competencies support systems thinking

In this section the context of food security is unpacked. Our aim is to identify a range of learning challenges surfaced by our analysis of this wicked problem. There is a lot to learn about systems thinking per se, and the more practice students get at it the better. But this is only part of the story. As we noted when we introduced the individual key competencies in Chapter 1, all the key competencies are always in play, combining with each other. Now it's time to add a range of other capabilities—that is, context-specific subsets of the key competencies—into the systems-thinking mix. If students are going to develop the dispositions to think

---

[7]. Complex systems also have a range of other properties that are beyond the scope of this chapter. Fritjof Capra's book *The Hidden Connections* provides a good introduction to complex systems and has a specific focus on how the brain learns (see Capra, 2002).

through and care about systems issues in our world, they need to be supported to become ready, willing, and able to do more than just think about connections between things and events—important as that may be.

To even begin to comprehend the challenges of ensuring everyone is adequately fed requires a special combination of critical and creative thinking. Critical thinking is needed to ask questions about the joined-up nature of food growing and distribution systems, and their relationship to economic and regulatory systems. Because many of the connections that hold these systems together will be hidden from everyday sight, a specific type of creative thinking is also called for. This is not the creativity of flights of fancy, but a more-grounded imagining of what is or what could be beyond our immediate experience. Here, critical and creative thinking provide two distinct faces to the same coin. Both are needed, in combination, for systems thinking.

Imaginative knowing is not just about knowledge-based aspects of thinking (i.e., cognition) however. It also has important emotional and aesthetic dimensions. The Steiner philosophy of schooling, for example, stresses the importance of the role played by the senses in stimulating and supporting acts of imagining. When building children's geographic imagination (such, for example, that they might begin to gain a feel for conditions of food production in far-off lands) Steiner teachers encourage children to explore many different visual materials, with "imagination-infused thinking" in the primary school years providing an important foundation for later independent rational thought.[8]

As the three dilemmas in Box 4.1 show, no one solution can be considered the correct and only answer to poor food security. So much depends on the values, assumptions, and specific interests that different people bring to the challenge of ensuring food security for all. Simple "it depends" thinking provides a good foundation for later, more abstract systems thinking, but this can bring its own challenges. In the Life Long Literacy project introduced in Chapter 3 (Box 3.1), some children

---

8. This idea comes from a paper in which Philip Wright discusses the developmental philosophy that underpins Steiner-Waldorf approaches to education, with an explicit focus on how geographical knowledge develops across the years of schooling (Wright, 2013).

had their sense of themselves as the first to know the "right" answer challenged by the more open-ended literary conversations that took place. "It depends" thinking is likely to pose dispositional challenges for children who are used to finding the right answer, because this way of thinking does not have the comforting certainty of one correct answer. An important aspect of the key competency of *managing self* is invoked here. Becoming more capable systems thinkers also requires learners to grow their resilience to respond positively to multiple possibilities and uncertainties. This is so when classes, schools, or communities include those who are fully food secure, and those who are not.

Learners' emotions are invoked in still more ways than those just outlined. Students who are fully food secure might experience the claim that they are taking (and wasting) more than their fair share of the world's available food as quite confronting. In this case, another aspect of *managing self* will need to be fostered. This is the capacity to withhold judgement by not immediately reacting negatively to implied criticism of one's own lifestyle. If students cannot learn to do this while still at school, as adults they might quickly dismiss or excuse any personal role in creating and sustaining wicked problems, and hence not be willing to consider their own citizenship responsibilities and possibilities.

We could label this as being open minded, but that doesn't seem to cover the emotional and highly personal nature of the reaction, thinking, and actions required. It seems likely that this dimension of *managing self* will need a lot of modelling, practice, and positive feedback if students are going to build up the disposition to voluntarily respond to suggested solutions for wicked problems in which they could well be on the losing end of any proposed redistribution of the world's resources. They also need to see that adults also take their own redistribution responsibilities seriously. As every teacher knows, young people display acute sensitivity towards hypocrisy and double standards.

We've already noted that *relating to others* has many dimensions, one of which is empathy—the ability to imaginatively and sensitively walk in each other's shoes. This aspect of *relating to others* comes sharply into focus when considering food security as a wicked problem, not least because it is a domestic issue as well as a global one. Students who are not food secure could easily be studying alongside those who are. And if not in the same school, they may not live so very far away in the same community. The challenge here is for students to see this issue from the perspective of others without judging them.

Laws governing the sale of perishable food can lead to a lot of waste. "Food rescue" services, such as Kaibosh in Wellington, collect and redistribute unsold but still edible food (for example, day-old bread) from retailers to those who need it most. Kaibosh lists on their website the following as the values that their volunteers need to bring to the work they do: courageous; compassionate; smart; genuine; and independent.[9] This seems like a pretty good manifesto for valuable dimensions of the key competencies of *managing self* and *relating to others* while *thinking* beyond one's personal advantages and interests.

Still another capability challenge lies in developing the capacity for understanding that one's own choices can have invisible consequences for others—and caring about this. This includes fostering the disposition to pay attention to, and care about, indirect as well as direct consequences of personal choices, now and in the future. Examples suggested by the food security articles we collected include:

- selecting sustainably grown food where there is a choice
- choosing to abide by food-gathering regulations as an ethical position (rather than, for example, acting from fear of being caught out)
- actively complying with biosecurity measures to help minimise ecological risks to food crops
- ethical shareholding, financial behaviours, and choices.

These choices are likely to be more costly to make than other available alternatives, and the alternatives will often be easier and more immediately rewarding default choices. Because they involve direct choices and actions, aspects of *participating and contributing* capabilities are invoked here.

---

9. Read more about their work at: http://www.kaibosh.org.nz/

Teaching that develops systems thinking

In the early years of schooling, teachers can lay a good foundation for systems thinking by helping children build a rich "library of experiences".[10] What children do matters here, alongside the shaping and enlarging of their experiences through rich conversations with more knowledgeable others. In the context of food security, experiences could encompass learning about: where our food comes from (locally and from other parts of the world); how it is produced, with associated environmental impacts; how it gets to distributors, food sellers, and then to us; what we do to make it good and safe to eat; and how it helps keep us healthy. Ultimately, all these pieces will need to be seen as interconnected if young people are to understand the challenge of feeding everyone as a systems issue.

Some interesting initiatives are designed to help children to join the dots between growing food locally, their own health, and the health of the planet. Here are just two:

- **Garden to Table** (http://www.gardentotable.org.nz) is a trust[11] that works with schools to help children experience the connections between growing, harvesting, preparing, cooking, and eating different foods. The practical hands-on focus is designed to ensure young people know what to do with fresh food, as opposed to being reliant on ready-prepared products. Eating together once the food has been prepared is an important part of the whole social and emotional experience. The initiative fosters the disposition to cook and eat a wide range of healthy foods.
- **Enviroschools** (http://www.enviroshools.org.nz) is another trust that is active in New Zealand schools. Their focus is on supporting schools to design and develop sustainable projects, with food growing as one of many possibilities. Children typically work alongside community volunteers to bring their project designs to

---

10. Science educator Ally Bull's working paper about what a "library of experiences" for young children might include can be found on NZCER's website: http://www.nzcer.org.nz/research/publications/library-experiences

11. This trust aims to work with adults in local communities, as well as school children.

fruition. The aim is to develop greater awareness of the impact of our living activities on the environment, and to develop children's dispositions to try and live more sustainably on our planet.

One "next challenge" lies in extending these local, and hence direct, experiences to other contexts that stimulate children's geographic imagination. An example that shows what might be possible comes from Jokikunta Primary School in Southern Finland. The children at this school teamed up with children from a school in Ecuador to exchange their experiences of sustainable gardening and food growing in their respective countries. To transcend language barriers, the children communicated by using drawings, photographs, and paintings. As one of the Finnish teachers noted, the "far away" world of Ecuador became real for the children as they exchanged experiences.[12] It's interesting to note that these activities were deliberately designed to be part of an investigation into the competencies needed to be and become a global citizen in an interconnected world.

Yet another challenge we might predict, given what we know about capability development in general, is that building academic insights into interconnections will be necessary but not sufficient to address the dispositional aspects of the capabilities described earlier in the chapter. The two examples that follow (Box 4.2) show how teachers can create rich learning opportunities that address dispositional challenges at the same time as they build knowledge and skills for *thinking* about the joined-up nature of events in the world.

The first example comes from a Year 12 home economics class, where food security is a specific focus topic. Here, the teacher has taught food security to a wide range of learners over a number of years, mostly in high-decile schools. Most of her students have had access to enough food. If they have experienced food security issues at all, these are more likely to have related to its "nutritional adequacy" (to quote one definition from the start of the chapter). The second example comes

---

12. To read more about this and other similar Finnish examples go to http://www.oph.fi/download/139354_Schools_reaching_out_to_a_global_world.pdf

from a unit of work for 11–14-year-old students. Its source is LENS science, which is the education outreach programme at the Liggins Institute at Auckland University.

Example 1

Provoking critical thinking in the context of food security

The lesson sequence begins with a deliberately provocative start. Students respond to a statement such as "New Zealand: A great place to bring up kids, right?" The spirited discussion opens up a space for the teacher to highlight hunger in families coping with unemployment and, increasingly, low wages but high living costs. The concept of food security now gains meaning for students, who are typically unaware of the term at the start of the unit of work.

To further provoke students' critical thinking the teacher uses activities such as a graffiti wall, where students respond to further provocative statements such as "If only they wouldn't keep having kids". Once the students' views and counterviews are out in the open, evidence-based resources are used to test assumptions against reality. (For example, demographic data shows that birth rates are only a little higher among Māori and Pasifika people, who are over-represented amongst the low-waged and unemployed.) Sometimes the teacher also uses cartoons with a food-security theme to provoke debate, but she finds that her students often need considerable support to read the subtleties of satire.[1]

Next students investigate how it can happen that people can't buy enough food to nourish their children. Topics debated include the various contributors to overall living costs, the miseries inflicted on desperate families by unregulated activities such as loan sharking, the reasons that many people can no longer grow their own basic food, and issues such as the waste generated by retailers' need to comply with strict food regulations. Through a series of more structured activities and open debates, the teacher aims to expand students' understanding

---

1. Making meaning from specialist forms of communication such as satirical cartoons is an important aspect of capabilities in *using language, symbols, and texts*.

Box 4.2: Creating rich learning opportunities to address dispositional challenges

of the many grey areas associated with poverty.

Finally, as an assessment exercise, students respond to an actual letter to the editor of a daily newspaper. The teacher chooses a recent example that expresses views typical of those many students hold at the start of the unit. They write a rebuttal letter suitable for publication in the same paper.

Example 2
Really caring about healthy eating

Scientists at the Liggins Institute research non-communicable diseases such as diabetes and heart disease. It is widely known that these types of diseases are linked to the sorts of food we eat over a longer period. Recently, the scientists have convincingly demonstrated that what mothers eat before and during pregnancy impacts on the health of their unborn child. More than this, those health impacts can be traced right through the child's life, into adulthood and even old age. Our health futures are set on track by what our mothers ate before we were born!

The educators at the Liggins have crafted this important work into a broad sequence of lessons for young adolescents. With local variations determined by their own teachers, the students:

- explore what non-communicable diseases are, and the risk factors that contribute to their occurrence
- work with real data from the Liggins research programme (suitably modified for accessibility) to find the evidence that supports the science claims
- engage with the scientists, via stories or in sessions where they can ask questions
- carry out an investigation into a question of their own that they have shaped as the unit unfolds
- prepare a talk or display about what they have learned, for a specific audience.

Across many schools the LENS educators have found that students really care

Box 4.2 (*continued*)

that babies can be affected by their mother's prenatal diet, with such far-reaching consequences. The research directs their critical attention to their own food choices in a way that more information-based lessons about healthy eating do not seem to do as powerfully. (None of us relish lecture-type advice that we don't really want to hear.) The researchers now have evidence that students who have studied this unit have: changed their own eating behaviours; talked at home about what they have learned; and, in some cases, been successful in proactively influencing their family's food buying habits in favour of healthier choices.

As well as this focus on making good personal choices in the present, this unit of work has a strong systems-thinking component. In this case, seemingly unconnected events are joined up across time to show the far-reaching consequences of healthy eating, not just for ourselves, but for generations yet to come.

Box 4.2 (*continued*)

Teachers create opportunities for competency development

The stories in this chapter draw attention to the importance of choices that skilful educators make on behalf of learners. It's true that students must be willing participants in allowing their competencies to be stretched and expanded. However, the ways in which teachers and other adults bring students to rich learning experiences—and support them—really do matter.

Curriculum choices matter. Often teachers seek to create engagement by allowing students a personal choice of learning topics. That is not the case in any of the examples outlined in this chapter. In all examples, teachers have drawn on their own deep curriculum knowledge to shape learning experiences that will draw students in by provoking their curiosity and engaging their emotions. In every case, there are immediate and longer term learning goals. The planned learning matters both for now and for the future.

Pedagogy matters. These teachers are willing to step outside their own comfort zones as they also plan to take the students out of theirs. Again, they must draw on their deep curriculum expertise, but not to shape and deliver right answers. Rather, they use their expertise to provoke and extend students' thinking (and their own) as more questions and problems open up to be confronted and explored.

Assessment and evaluation matters. While it is only minimally addressed in this chapter (and indeed in the book as a whole) it should also be apparent that evidence of capability development is unlikely to emerge from traditional pen-and-paper recall tasks. This is not to say formal written tasks are not relevant, but where they are used they cannot look for one right answer. With systems issues, there is unlikely to be only one correct response. Creative assessment thinking is needed to find ways to document students' action responses to their growing awareness of, and insights into, how systems work in the world, and the possibilities and limitations of their own choices and actions in response. One theorist said that the most important assessment question we can ask is "what does it mean to know?"[13] Consider how each story highlights the meaning that the teacher wanted students to take from their new knowing, and what they looked for as evidence of that new meaning-making.

Capabilities are embedded within the idea of competency

This chapter has foregrounded systems thinking as a specific type of *thinking* capability needed by future-oriented learners. Along the way, various other capabilities associated with the other key competencies have also come into view. These are summarised in Table 4.1.

As we also showed in the previous chapter, it will be obvious that this division of capabilities among four key competencies is arbitrary to some extent. The key competencies overlap and merge when brought to bear on real issues, in real contexts. As just one example, "learning to manage uncertainty, recognising instances where there can be no one 'right' answer" could equally well have been placed under *thinking*, because it is integral to developing systems-thinking capabilities.

---

13. This question comes from "Assessment as Inquiry", a seminal paper by Ginette Delandshere about the need to rethink our assessment models and assumptions (Delandshere, 2002).

Table 4.1: Capabilities for systems thinking

Key competency	Associated capabilities to be fostered
Thinking	<ul><li>"It depends" thinking; thinking beyond immediate events and connections; creative thinking; critical thinking.</li><li>Open-mindedness; critical reflection.</li></ul>
Relating to others	<ul><li>Empathy; non-judgemental recognition of how others are situated.</li></ul>
Managing self	<ul><li>Willingness critically to confront own actions and impacts of own choices.</li><li>Developing self-awareness of how personal values influence our thinking and choices.</li><li>Learning to manage uncertainty, recognising instances where there can be no one "right" answer.</li></ul>
Participating and contributing	<ul><li>Making considered choices; taking action in ways that address identified issues.</li></ul>

We can see from the examples that teaching for this rich combination of capabilities is likely to entail:
- **joining-up seemingly unconnected things or events** to encourage thinking about less-obvious connections (across events, places, time, or a combination of all)

- **exploring systems as parts and wholes**, and the dynamic relationships between these
- **engaging and exploring students' emotions**, not just their rational thinking
- **surfacing students' values and assumptions**, to explore why they think and act as they do
- **exploring evidence for claims**—not taking them at face value
- **exploring different potential choices and solutions**, emphasising that there is not necessarily one right answer or solution to an issue, and that different courses of action will impact differentially on different groups of people.

Complex systems challenges bring many problems, not least of them knowing who to trust when information emerges in so many different combinations, from so many different sources, and without any overall imposed authority. This is itself a wicked problem, and becomes even more so when wicked problems are the objects of inquiry! The next chapter addresses this challenge.

5
Learning who to trust when knowledge claims conflict

CO_2 levels head into unknown territory

Drought plan "lacking climate change forethought"

**CLIMATE CHANGE SCEPTIC
rejects criticism as "hate speech"**

CLIMATE CRISIS BREWS FOR COFFEE

Figure 5.1: News media headlines

A focus on meaning-making

THIS CHAPTER TAKES THE wicked problem of climate change as its starting point. Here, the key competencies we bring to the fore are *thinking* and *using language, symbols, and texts*. We discuss learning challenges that are focused on meaning-making and the nature of subjects.

The constellations of capabilities required to address learning challenges related to the nature of subjects are often called literacies—for example, science literacy, media literacy, or statistical literacy. We'll show how and why students need to learn to talk the talk (or use the discourses) of the relevant discipline area(s). As we do so, we'll need to delve into some areas related to the philosophy of knowledge. None of us (the authors) experienced a specific focus on philosophy within the subjects we chose for our own initial tertiary education and we expect the same will be true for some of our readers. This lack of familiarity can make some of the ideas seem hard at first. Stick with us, and we hope all will be clear by the end of the chapter.

The wicked problem of climate change is relatively easy to define, but what we should do about it is not straightforward. Scientists say the composition of the atmosphere is changing in ways that are causing the planet to get warmer. This has potentially disastrous consequences for: different ecosystems; the growing of food crops; low-lying land (water expands as it gets warmer); places prone to violent weather (a warmer atmosphere contains more energy, which fuels fiercer storms); the availability of fresh water (changes to weather patterns can cause droughts), and so on. It will be obvious that all these are systems issues. They are likely to interact with each other in many different ways. All have the potential to trigger other sets of challenges which are not hard to imagine. For example, where will all the people go if some very large cities become uninhabitable because of food, water supply, or flooding issues?[1]

---

1. New Zealand's Chief Scientist recently commissioned a report that explored the changes New Zealand is likely to experience, and to discuss the sorts of adaptations to we are likely to need to make to our way of life: http://www.pmcsa.org.nz/wp-content/uploads/New-Zealands-Changing-Climate-and-Oceans-report.pdf (Office of the Prime Minister's Science Advisory Committee, 2013).

Not everyone agrees that the problem really does exist, and that these cascades of consequences are likely to happen. Climate-change scientists say that evidence is convincing that humans have caused changes in the atmosphere, and that these changes are causing the planet to warm. They say we need to make urgent changes in our lifestyles to try and slow the damage as quickly as we can. By contrast, some commentators and lobbyists work to convince governments and citizens that climate change is a naturally occurring phenomenon. It is not caused by our activities, and therefore is something we cannot do anything about, or need to worry ourselves about. Some other people deny that it is happening at all.

With debates about climate change as the context, this chapter discusses the capabilities students need to develop to make sense of contested knowledge claims. Who are students to believe? For that matter, who are adults to believe? Can teachers help students, over the years of their schooling, learn ways to know who to trust and why? There are quite a few dimensions to take into account when thinking about this challenge. Take, for example, the idea that our mental models for knowledge are not serving us so well in this century (see Chapter 3). The assumption that knowledge is true, stable, discipline-specific stuff, developed slowly over time by experts, underpins traditional models of teaching and learning. This mental model is so familiar from the education most of us experienced as to be invisible to our conscious thinking. However, this invisibility turns out to be something that can be used against us, without us necessarily realising it is happening.

Let's use a concrete example that shows what can happen when our trust in "expert" knowledge is abused. Box 5.1 briefly summarises the main ways in which the claims of many scientists are countered by climate-change sceptics, some of whom are also scientists. The strategies summarised there show how the widespread but tacit mental model of knowledge as true, stable stuff has been used in several different ways, with considerable success, to unsettle knowledge claims about climate change in the public mind. One reason that these strategies work so well is that even those scientists who do think that we should be concerned about climate change cannot say for sure what will happen—only what they think is most likely to happen, on the balance of probabilities, given due attention to matters of risk assessment, and given that there will always be areas where more knowledge is still needed.

How might teachers help students to think more critically about knowledge claims given these complexities? One expert on critical thinking recently said that students need to learn how to play "hidden games" of learning.[2] Instead of being asked to accept ready-packaged knowledge at face value, they need to learn ways to think critically about where knowledge comes from and what gives it authority. We investigate how teachers might do that in this chapter.

In Chapter 4 we saw that one person's solution can be another's problem when people bring different sets of values and assumptions to the social dimensions of wicked problems. It's no surprise, then, that there might appear to be winners and losers when the climate changes. One well-known strategy used by climate change deniers is cherry-picking convenient aspects of climate change (see Box 5.1). As we've already seen, students need to learn to step back and see multiple dimensions to an issue; and teachers need to acknowledge the lack of a single right solution when relevant. This chapter integrates that specific type of capability with some powerful new ideas about knowledge and knowing. But first there is also one really big challenge that we need to put on the table, with full awareness of its complexities and potential pitfalls.

⁂

---

2. David Perkins is a Harvard-based expert on developing children's thinking capabilities. His recent book, *Making Learning Whole*, distils findings from a number of research projects to develop the metaphor that "whole learning" is about teaching children how to play "junior versions" of authentic knowledge-building activities in the world (Perkins, 2009).

Strategies used to deny or explain away climate change

This set of strategies comes via the Hot Topic website[1] and has been drawn from the book titled *Climate Change Denial: Heads in the Sand* (see Washington & Cook, 2011).

Conspiracy theories: For example, "Climategate". This media scandal centred on a series of email communications between several groups of scientists. The scientists said they were discussing how best to represent their data so it could be understood by the public. Climate-change sceptics claimed the messages between the scientists were evidence that they were conspiring to create misleading data sets.

Quoting fake experts: The British peer Lord Monckton, who toured New Zealand at the start of 2013, is a climate-change sceptic. He is not a climate-change scientist but used his social status in the United Kingdom to lend authority to his personal views about climate change. Climate-change scientists said he had no authority to make knowledge claims in their expert area and should not be using his status to do this. As the headline at the start of this chapter shows, Lord Monckton deflected critique of his arguments as personal attacks on him—and of course there was a personal element because of the way he was using his personal status.

Impossible expectations: This strategy involves sceptics saying that scientists should be certain before we need to listen to their knowledge claims, and that they should be in total agreement with one another. Scientists say they cannot and will not give such assurances of certainty. The central endeavour of science is to doubt and test knowledge claims to ensure their robustness. Doubting and debating comes with the territory. The uncertainties of complex systems change provide a further complication (see Chapter 4). Because outcomes of complex systems are emergent and unpredictable, certainty about climate changes is impossible, no matter how well scientists do their work.

Misrepresentations and logical fallacies: Some sceptics claim that the

---

1. http://hot-topic.co.nz/climate-change-denial-heads-in-the-sand. This is a website that regularly brings news about climate change to a New Zealand audience.

Box 5.1: Strategies used to deny or explain away climate change

climate changes happening now must be natural because the climate has changed in the past. Scientists would certainly agree that the climate has changed in the past but argue that the logic of this argument is flawed. For example, it assumes that all instances of climate change will have the same underlying causes. In cases like this, sceptics call on common-sense ideas and experiences to support knowledge claims. This poses real challenges for scientists because their rebuttals are often counterintuitive and harder to understand.

Cherry-picking evidence: Sceptics might say, for example, that a colder winter than usual is evidence that warming can't be happening. Again they draw on common-sense experiences to look for seeming exceptions and counter-examples. Scientists would say that all the relevant evidence must be considered, not just selective parts. For them, counter-examples need to be carefully explored for what they might teach us that we don't yet know. They should be taken as opportunities for knowledge-building, not confirmation of existing views.

Box 5.1 (*continued*)

Avoiding the impression that "anything goes and nothing matters"

As adults, our experiences in life have helped us understand that different people will inevitably bring different points of view and values to social issues. These differences impact on how all of us make personal meaning and think about solutions. Scientists are no different from anyone else in this regard. Just like everyone else, they bring their personal values and social contexts to their work. (Some have a vested interest in the commercial usefulness of their investigations, for example.)

There is, however, only one planet, with one atmosphere, and one complex interconnected set of weather systems. For these physical systems, the most critical test of what is true is what actually happens. Ultimately, planet Earth will change, regardless of what we think we know. As we saw in Chapter 4, complex-systems theory predicts that big changes might well be sudden and irreversible. This really ups the ante when it comes to deciding whose knowledge claims to trust. Should we come to the point of knowing we were wrong to ignore the escalating evidence of climate change, it will almost certainly be too late to scale back on the factors that many people now hold to blame for it happening.

One clear implication of all this is that everyone needs to learn when to trust experts, and understand the reasons why. Some knowledge claims will be important to take seriously, and some won't, but how do people tell these apart? In particular, how do we learn to tell when our views are being manipulated, for whatever motive? How might each of us develop a critical radar for truth claims? With students' futures in mind, how do teachers help them to know when it is important to doubt and when they can afford to trust?[3] How do teachers help students discern when trusting is the wiser option, even if there are some doubts, if the risks of being wrong are too high? And how do we do all this without causing our young people to lose hope for their futures, or to sink into deep cynicism about everyone and everything?

These questions should not be read as a purely personal challenge, although all of us do have to make personal decisions about truth claims from time to time. Many social institutions work to distil truth claims and make critical decisions on our behalf. Courts of law are one example, and with occasional exceptions they enjoy high public trust in New Zealand.[4] The trust we place in other institutions is more problematic. Governments and politicians, for example, tend to rate poorly on matters of trust, although they too are intended—in principle—to work in ways that weigh up competing interests and knowledge claims to determine courses of action that are in the best public good. The media also play a critical role in shaping what the public see and believe, with

---

3. Stephen Norris is a science educator researcher who has written about this challenge. He points out that we need to know when to trust the expertise of others in many situations (when getting something repaired, when visiting a health professional and so on). If we don't discriminate between when we can and can't trust we risk becoming crippled by "pathological doubt" (see Norris, 1997, p. 250).

4. It's interesting that jurisprudence—the system of practices used to establish legal truths in Western courts of law—emerged from the deliberations of a school of philosophers known as the American pragmatists. In the wake of the American civil war, these deep thinkers were looking for new ways to understand how we come to know the world and to determine matters of truth. John Dewey, who is well known as an education reformer, was a member of this group (to find out more see Menand, 2002).

varying degrees of critical thinking and trust. We don't have space to address all of these contexts in this chapter. What we can do is lay out some ideas about how to raise students' awareness that who they choose to trust, and on what grounds, is an area where they need to develop their capabilities to make critical but well-informed decisions.

Deepening insights about knowledge and meaning-making
The key competencies we foreground in this chapter are *thinking* and *using language, symbols, and texts*. For the types of learning experiences we are about to discuss, they are indivisible faces of the same coin.

When *NZC* was first being developed, *using language, symbols, and texts* was, for a time, given the title of *meaning making*. People who rejected this title quite possibly thought about the scope of meaning-making only in terms of the personal understandings students make of their learning experiences. This framing could be seen as positioning meaning-making as learning-as-usual. Who doesn't hope that students will understand what they are taught? As an alternative to this traditional view, consider the impact of reframing the idea of *using language, symbols, and texts* so that meaning-making is seen to also include thinking critically about public knowledge (that is, more than purely personal knowledge). This broader focus brings a much more challenging framing of the key competency into view. Public knowledge invokes questions about important philosophical matters such as truth, belief, and evidence.[5] And as we've just outlined, truth, belief and evidence are precisely the matters that lie at the heart of debates about whether climate change is actually happening. We could have taken any wicked problem and produced a similar analysis of its public-knowledge claims and counterclaims.

---

5. This list comes from Hugh Sockett, an American professor of education. In his recent book *Knowledge and Virtue in Teaching and Learning: The Primacy of Dispositions*, he argues that children should be exposed to the messy uncertainties of making public-knowledge claims from the very beginnings of school, and that if we do not do this we are guilty of keeping important "epistemological secrets" from our young people (Sockett, 2012). This argument resonates with David Perkins' idea of supporting children to play the "hidden games" of learning (Perkins, 2009).

With hindsight it seems a pity that the title *meaning making* was eventually rejected. An opportunity was lost to signal some important ideas about knowledge. *Meaning making* makes more sense (and different sense) as a title for this key competency if we have public knowledge in our sights. We now dig a little deeper into this idea.

The characteristics of public knowledge

Describing subject areas such as history, science, and mathematics as *disciplines* signals something really important about the way they build public knowledge. People who make public-knowledge claims (for example, scientists, historians, mathematicians, and so forth) are expected to adhere to professional norms in a disciplined way. This discipline involves making every possible effort to set aside personal (subjective) interests to be as impartial (objective) as possible. It is not easy to do—if it was, these experts wouldn't need to be so rigorous in their work. No one can ever be totally objective, and sometimes experts do make claims that are knowingly dishonest in some aspect. But they usually get found out sooner rather than later.

People who make public-knowledge claims are expected to follow established knowledge-building conventions in their area, or to justify why they have not.[6] Some conventions will relate to how evidence is gathered and presented. The inquiry processes followed must be openly set out and be convincing to other experts in the relevant field. Other conventions will relate to how new evidence builds from and contributes further to already-validated knowledge in the field (that is, its established theories and concepts). Still other conventions might relate to how meaning is shaped and conveyed when new knowledge is communicated (that is, the types of representations that are used by experts in a discipline area).

To learn about conventions for shaping evidence, justifying claims, and representing ideas is to learn about how meaning is made in a

---

6. When new inquiry methods are devised, whole new fields of knowledge-building can be opened up. These new ways of inquiring will gradually develop their own robust conventions as they become established and validated.

discipline. *NZC* signals that these knowledge-building conventions are things that students ought to learn about. The Science learning area, for example, has an overarching Nature of Science strand that is supposed to be woven through the content strands. History has a specific focus on historical thinking, drawing on important concepts such as historical significance, historical perspectives, cause and consequence, and sources of evidence.[7] This focus on the nature of subjects takes us back to the idea of discourses which was introduced in Chapter 3. Students need to learn what is involved in talking scientists' talk—or the talk of any other discipline.

One really tricky challenge here is that the meaning of some words in discipline-based discourses can be very different from the meaning these very same words assume in everyday discourse. A classic example of this is the word *theory*. In science, a theory is an overarching explanation that ties together all the currently known phenomena and concepts of a specific inquiry area.[8] It is as close as scientists will go to calling something an established fact. (As we've already noted, new evidence might shift understandings, so scientists will never say they are 100 percent certain.) Contrast this with the meaning conveyed by the everyday phrase "I have a theory that ... " This means a best guess, based on our current experience and private knowledge. This is a good-enough guide for routine daily life, but it is a personal theory not a public one. Students do need to learn to tell the difference, and to know why this difference matters.

Now think about a time when you and someone else were talking at cross purposes. Our own understandings and experiences bring words to life for us in uniquely personal ways, and it often takes a while to

---

7. The web/blog site of Canadian history educator Peter Seixas (http://historicalthinking.ca/) has a front-page discussion of six important historical thinking concepts. For New Zealand-based examples of what developing these in the classroom might look like, the book *History Matters* is a useful reference (Harcourt & Sheehan, 2012).
8. A recent book by complexity theorist Brent Davis looked at how different metaphors for teaching relate to different theories of knowledge. This book began in an unexpected way—by discussing the scientific theory of evolution. This theory continues to be controversial in some religions precisely because of its meaning-making power. It explains so many different phenomena that it changed how philosophers have thought about knowledge-building and knowing ever since (see Davis, 2004).

figure out what's happening when we miscommunicate. By contrast, the discipline areas use established meaning-making conventions so that people who know how to use the relevant discourse are less likely to talk past one another. This does not just apply to words, or even the way strings of words are put together to convey meaning (that is, the grammatical conventions of a discipline). Arrows, for example, convey very different meanings in a flow chart (this leads to that); a ray diagram (the path followed by one hypothetical particle of light); and a food chain (the direction of energy flow). An equals sign in arithmetic means "and the total is", whereas in algebra the very same sign means "both sides of the equation are equivalent". Other aspects of diagrams and equations have their own conventions in different discipline areas, as do models and other images used to convey meanings.

All social settings have their own meaning-making conventions. In some settings, gestures convey meanings wordlessly (refereeing signals or dance moves are examples of this). Symbols of all types do the same, and so do systems of symbols (for example, the markings on a playing field in combination with refereeing conventions and the specific meanings given to words). Sometimes people in search of new meanings will deliberately jumble up established ways of making meaning, trying to prompt people to see with new eyes (successful modern art does this). All these meaning-making systems work to the extent that everyone who needs to know understands what is being conveyed. Being able to recognise and use all types of relevant meaning-making conventions is an important aspect of learning about the nature of a subject, and hence within scope for developing capabilities in *thinking* and *using language, symbols, and texts*.

In summary then, meaning-making within a discipline encompasses all the:
- context-specific meanings given to symbols, words, and phrases (which might have different meanings in other contexts)
- ways in which words, images, and symbols are shaped and combined to represent ideas within the discipline

- rules which everyone working within the discipline follows to build and justify new knowledge claims.

In all these areas students need to build their discipline-specific literacies (such as science literacy, statistical literacy, and the like) so that they can use the relevant discourses in appropriate ways. These literacies enable new learning, and they allow students to convey what they know and understand. They also give them access to critical insights needed to check public-knowledge claims against standards of truth and evidence, so they can decide who to believe when knowledge claims conflict.

What might a focus on meaning-making look like in the classroom?

The following examples (Box 5.2) illustrate different ways that teachers might bring discipline-based meaning-making into focus for students. What the examples have in common is an intention to help students learn how matters of probable truth are established in public discourses. We begin with a science example, followed by two examples that combine media studies with a discipline area (science and social sciences respectively). The fourth example foregrounds the use of an arts-based pedagogy to explore a complex issue where the different aspects of public knowledge come directly into conflict.

Example 1

Learning to make meaning of scientists' texts

This example is set in a Year 13 biology class in a suburban school. While investigating the question of whether 1080 poison should be used for possum control, some students found an eight-page science paper that was highly relevant, but initially looked quite daunting to read. Their teacher made copies of this paper so that the class could work on it together. The class began with the abstract (a feature that the teacher had previously found students did not know how to use). They discussed the general purpose served by abstracts and then the specific content to determine its potential relevance to their work.

Box 5.2: Four examples of discipline-based meaning making

The next step was to record the reference correctly on the top of a dot jot summary sheet, which encourages students to get into the habit of recording this data systematically. Students then tackled the main text of the article. They initially read through it together and, where necessary, the teacher reminded them about strategies for tackling words that they did not know. For example, they might read on to see if the meaning could be inferred from what followed. They might discuss places on the internet or people they might go to for help. Because the paper addressed multiple aspects of the issue they were exploring, the teacher then encouraged the students to pick one focus (for example, the effect of 1080 on mammals) and look for all the relevant information to summarise on the dot jot sheet.

The teacher said that being critical about sources is something that students can find hard to do without a clear focus on what to look for, and why. They began by looking critically at the references. The teacher reminded them about the function these serve and what they tell the reader about the quality of the argument they have just summarised. They also checked for evidence that the journal where the paper was published is peer reviewed, and the teacher reminded them why that is important. Where possible they then used the internet to check on authors whose work was strongly represented. Who were they? Who did they work for, and what sort of work did they do?

Example 2

Is there such a thing as healthy chocolate?

This example is set in a Year 11 science class in a secondary school in a different area of New Zealand. Right at the start of the school year, the students in this class looked at an advertisement for "healthy chocolate".[1] Their teacher asked them to discuss whether they trusted the claims made in this advertisement. They were encouraged to justify their decisions and record their thoughts on whiteboards, sticky notes, or electronic forums. The teacher then gave the

---

1. This activity can be found at http://www.upd8.org.uk. The link is in the right-hand sidebar of "most popular" activities. You will need to register to download it but it is free to do so.

Box 5.2 (*continued*)

students some evidence behind the claim. They had to sort and interpret this for themselves, and then revisit the advertisement to consider their original decision. Had it changed or stayed the same? Why or why not?

In small groups, students then used a framework provided by the teacher to build a checklist of things to look for in trustworthy science. They then applied the checklist to a range of case studies to evaluate the science behind claims. Once they had some confidence with the checklist, the teacher gave them an article outlining the science behind the claim "healthy heart chocolate" and asked them to evaluate this article using their checklist. When they had done this, students revisited their decision about whether to trust the advertisement.

The checklist that students developed during this activity was subsequently used as they developed their own investigations. The teacher continued to challenge them to explain why she should trust their conclusions, using the language developed for the checklist. In subsequent NCEA assessments of students' own investigations, the majority of Year 11 students were able to develop valid methods and evaluate their methods with specific reference to ideas within the checklist. The following year, the teacher observed these same students vigorously debating the methods they had devised for investigations. They were confident in their understanding of the nature of science investigations, and able to express and justify their opinions, and reflect on their methodology.

Example 3
Learning how "truth" is established in and by news-making

This example is set in an urban secondary school close to a city centre. A social studies teacher said that his Year 10 students often have an intuitive sense that objectivity is desirable, but find it difficult to understand that there is no such thing as a single, simple, uncontested, and final "truth" in the news. He designed a unit that focused on the role of the media in society to try and teach his students the tentative nature of knowledge and truth. A specific challenge was that he did not want them to descend into what he described as "a relativistic anything goes" attitude. At the same time, he was well aware that some media reporting is

Box 5.2 (*continued*)

better than others. He wanted his students to learn to tell the difference, and he knew that they could only begin to do that by exploring how matters of truth do get established as news is being made.

With this big goal in mind, the unit he developed had three key components. First, students working in small groups produced their own piece of investigative journalism on an issue they felt was significant to the school or the local community. Right from the start, being asked to choose something that was "significant" (a historical thinking concept) produced a lot of debate about how and why our knowledge of events can only ever be a partial selection from all the events that vie for our attention. The developed accounts were published on a website, and the details were distributed via the school newsletter and in local letter boxes. There were structured opportunities to reflect on the challenges that arose, and to focus on how creating the news was meaning-making.

Next, the students worked to describe the role of the media in a democratic society like New Zealand. They read and considered material on the Te Ara website that addresses this topic.[2] Discussion of the idea of a "fourth estate" and its role in a democracy led to a small case-study that probed a topical controversy that directly involved the media. This issue centred on the relationships between the Defence Force and the Government Communications Security Bureau (a government security agency), and comments made by these groups that framed the media as subversive, and therefore a risk to be managed, rather than an important group with whom to interact more openly. To expand students' awareness of the impact of media on their lives even further, the teacher selected several TED talks from a collection called "Media with meaning".[3] This was an

---

2. This material can be found at http://www.teara.govt.nz/en/media-and-politics/page-1. Notice how the central relationship between media and democracy is expanded within a broader systems framing, showing how events, structure, and processes that might otherwise seem unconnected can come together in this space.

3. Go to http://www.ted.com/playlists/21/media_with_meaning.html. As an illustrative example, the first talk by E-Bay millionaire Jeff Skoll explores the power for good that can come from deliberately leveraging pro-social media stories that give people hope or that raise critical issues for wider public debate. For example, his media group was responsible for the conversion of Al Gore's slide show into the widely watched and debated movie *An Inconvenient Truth*, which addresses climate change.

Box 5.2 (*continued*)

important addition. The focus of these talks is on the use of media, including film and television, to develop and share positive visions of futures we could work towards, and of the difference that individuals and groups can make.

Finally small groups of students developed a role play of a news report commemorating 10 years since the invasion of Iraq. The teacher gave each group a specific political perspective within which to develop their report. As they watched one another's role plays the students were able to directly experience how perspective can change the way the same set of events might be seen by different groups. Together, the three components of the unit provided the basis for discussions and reflection on the idea of truth and evidence in the news.

Example 4
Should the wild horses in the Kaimanawa be culled?
This Years 5 and 6 class in a large, urban primary school was guided through an exploration of "truth/s and enviro-ethics". The phrase in quote marks comes from the title of a book chapter, written by Viv Aitken, in the book *Connecting Curriculum, Linking Learning*.[4] The chapter illustrates how using the arts-based pedagogy known as "Mantle of the Expert" can support curriculum integration. Children had to confront both sides of the emotive issue of whether to cull wild horses. Unavoidable tensions between different courses of action were progressively unfolded through various drama activities.

The unit began by exploring the issue from the perspective of wanting to keep all the horses alive. The teachers[5] were well aware that love of animals such as horses would be an emotional hook to draw the children deep into the overall learning experience. Via a series of drama activities led by the teachers,

---

4. *Connecting Curriculum, Linking Learning* explores curriculum integration, with a focus on arts-based pedagogies including the Mantle of the Expert. The book was written by Deborah Fraser, Viv Aitken and Barbara Whyte from the University of Waikato (Fraser, Aitken, & Whyte, 2013). The brief account in our chapter is paraphrased from their more detailed account, which is well worth reading in full.
5. The classroom teacher worked with an expert from the University of Waikato, and several student teachers were also involved.

Box 5.2 (*continued*)

> the children were drawn into the perspective of a protest group called "Wild and Free" who were opposed to the culling of wild horses. Next, a quite different series of activities saw one teacher take on the mantle of a Department of Conservation scientist, who led the children through a series of science investigations designed to help them develop an understanding of the unique ecology of the area. (Being alpine desert, this ecosystem is fragile and easily damaged if the horse population grows too big.) At this point the children had to face the tension between protecting the native flora and fauna of the Kaimanawa alpine area and protecting the introduced horses.
>
> The overall framing for bringing these opposed courses of action into direct juxtaposition was that the children were researchers for a documentary company called "Problem Solving People" whose mission was to be an honest company with integrity. In this way the design of the unit shone a positive spotlight on the construction of media accounts of issues, without shying away from the ethical tensions that such companies inevitably face. The children produced storyboards for a documentary about the issue, but did not actually create their documentary. This decision was taken to keep the focus of the unit firmly on the ethical issues being explored.

Box 5.2 (*continued*)

Subject-specific capabilities in *using language, symbols, and texts*

Examples 1–4 in Box 5.2 give students valuable practice in critical thinking about knowledge claims. The discourses of the relevant disciplines are drawn on because of their important role in meaning-making, but they are not necessarily the direct focus of the intended learning. Specific ways in which disciplines make meaning also need to be brought directly to students' attention. The examples show one way this could happen in the Science learning area.

Five "science capabilities" were recently developed to support the Science learning area of *NZC*. They show how the Nature of Science strand might act to refocus more traditional teaching and learning, with students' growing capabilities for informed citizenship in mind.

(As we noted in Chapter 2, *NZC* identifies this as the overarching purpose for learning science.) The science capabilities were distilled from international research that discusses Nature of Science ideas which should be developed in schools. Deceptively simple names were chosen for them: "Gather and interpret information"; "Use evidence to support ideas"; "Critique evidence"; "Make meaning of scientific representations"; and "Engage with science". Think about the challenges of sifting the wheat from the chaff in debates about climate change. How might robust capabilities in each of these named areas help?

A suite of resources was developed as part of the capabilities project. These illustrate how science-capability development could be supported from Years 1 to 10.[9] Each resource shows how to adapt an existing resource to foreground a dimension of capability. The question "what's important here?" is used to show how this learning target could make a contribution to students' overall citizenship capability development. Here are selections from the "what's important here?" part of three resources that support the capability "Make meaning of scientific representations":

> Scientists write about their observations and research with enough detail for others to be able to critique what they have done. Descriptions in science tend to be factual and objective. Students need practice to be able to describe things in this particular way. (Level 1/2 resource based on materials in *Standing Up: Skeletons and Frameworks, Building Science Concepts, Book 51*.[10])
>
> Scientists represent their ideas in a variety of ways, including models, graphs, charts, diagrams and written texts. At this level, the important thing is to focus students' attention on the fact that different representations have different purposes, and scientists choose the best way of clearly

---

9. Development of these resources was funded by New Zealand's Ministry of Education. They are freely available on Science Online: http://scienceonline.tki.org.nz/New-resources-to-support-science-education.
10. The 64 titles in the *Building Science Concepts* series are listed at http://scienceonline.tki.org.nz/What-do-my-students-need-to-learn/Building-Science-Concepts/Titles-and-concept-overviews

illustrating an idea. All models are similar in some ways and different in some ways to the thing they represent. (Level 3/4 resource based on materials in *Spring is a Season, Building Science Concepts, Book 44*.)

Scientists represent their ideas in a variety of ways, including models, graphs, charts, diagrams, written texts—and the measurement scales they use. Students need to understand that scientific scales have been deliberately constructed for specific purposes, and can be refined over time as they are used for these purposes. However this does not mean that "anything goes"—understanding how critique and consensus building are used to impart authority to such scales is an important aspect of building science literacy. (Level 5 resource based on two versions of the Modified Mercalli Scale which measures the felt effects of earthquakes.)

An important next step is to build a rich body of practical experience around the use of these resources, and to address important questions about what making progress in capability development might look like for students of different ages. After at least 12 resources had been developed for each capability, the team looked across them to distil key differences between the sort of learning opportunities that might support capability development for younger and older students.

Opportunities to develop meaning-making capabilities

These classroom stories and new teacher resources all show how and why the teacher's curriculum intentions and pedagogy make an important contribution to students' opportunities to extend and strengthen their capabilities. While aspects of the key competencies of *thinking* and *using language, symbols, and texts* have been a specific focus of this chapter, important aspects of all the other key competencies were in play.

The teachers in Examples 1–4 (Box 5.2) all helped students to slowly and purposefully build their awareness of why it might be impossible to find one "right" answer to complex social issues. Students needed to stand in the shoes of others to understand why different people might think and act as they do. Once again, fostering empathy was an important consideration in strengthening the key competency *relating to others*. Importantly, the teachers also supported this growing awareness of different perspectives with critical reflection strategies. For example, ethical thinking and values clarification were a focus of learning where relevant.[11]

Each teacher designed rich and engaging learning experiences that would hook students into the learning. Their curiosity was aroused. They were encouraged to be problem finders, as well as problem solvers. To be successful at problem finding, students need to think beyond the given learning context and tasks. Obviously being curious is a good place to start. In Chapter 4 we saw how a specific type of creative thinking, grounded in what might be, can also be in play when students need to think beyond what they already know. Doing this type of thinking takes considerable intellectual effort and requires learners to be independent thinkers. They need to be able to access thinking skills (such as those needed for systems thinking), and to draw on relevant knowledge so that their thinking does not stray too far beyond the workable boundaries of the task.

Notice too, the strong dispositional component in these activities. You can't make someone be curious. You can't make them be an independent thinker. But you also can't corral their thinking if they are determined to set off on wild flights of fancy that have nothing constructive to add to the task. All conditions mentioned here require considerable self-discipline, and hence provide opportunities to strengthen and stretch capabilities in *managing self*.

In these classrooms, the deliberate provocation of strong feelings was also designed to foster students' dispositions to be the sort of people who want to seek out the truth(s) at the heart of the questions they were exploring. Hooking students in is critically important if we hope to foster students' dispositions to be and become critical seekers of truth, evidence, and power in public knowledge. Taking knowledge claims

---

11. Some tools to support the development of ethical thinking frameworks can be found on the Biotechnology Learning Hub: http://www.biotechlearn.org.nz/themes/bioethics/using_ethical_frameworks_in_the_classroom

at face value is our default pathway though life. To be a more critical thinker takes a special combination of know-how and willingness. It is hard work, and sometimes not very comfortable. Again, students have to want to do it for themselves when the classroom requirement to do so is no longer present. In this way, strengthening capabilities in *managing self* has immediate and longer term implications for ongoing learning.

With age-appropriate differences, the teaching and learning experiences described in these stories included various combinations of carefully supported classroom conversations about how we (in the collective sense) know what we know.[12] Matters of truth, belief, and evidence were a direct focus for learning conversations. These teachers did not shy away from controversy and spirited debate. However, debate in these cases did not amount to an anything-goes free-for-all. Instead, the nature and sequencing of the learning activities supported and encouraged careful consideration of, and critical thinking about, opposing perspectives and truth claims. These learning conditions supported a powerful combination of open-mindedness and intellectual honesty, modelled by the teacher and practised by everyone. Again, it will be evident that dispositions to "be" certain types of people in the world were being fostered alongside growth in knowledge and skills.

Participating and contributing also had a strong presence in these classrooms, both in immediate learning, and in developing capabilities for the future. There were opportunities for students to practice being critical meaning-makers, not just uncritical recipients of meaning made by others. As they learned about the role of disciplines in building trustworthy knowledge—with associated practice in using disciplinary conventions—they experienced what it feels like to be a scientist, a historian, a reporter, and so on.

The questions or issues at the heart of these units were rich with possibilities to explore knowledge claims. This type of exploration leads to naturally occurring integration across learning areas, or across

---

12. The theoretical term for a deliberate focus on how we know what we know is epistemic thinking. The word *epistemic* comes from epistemology, which is a branch of philosophy that considers how truth claims are established.

disciplines within a learning area (for example, media studies and history are both disciplines within the umbrella of the social sciences).

Where to next?

Our aim in writing this chapter has been to open up a space for professional conversations about the nature of meaning-making in different learning areas, and how educators can support students to learn about the work of the different disciplines. We've used the context of climate change to show why we think that doing this ought to be an important aspect of students' overall key competency development. There is much for education professionals to discuss:

- How can educators (and interested others) foster students' dispositions to want to be critical seekers of truth(s) in the world?
- What might be the consequences if this is not done?
- How do the different disciplines contribute to students' knowledge-seeking capabilities? (What overlaps, and what is unique?)
- At what age would it be appropriate to start?
- How might our young people be encouraged to stay hopeful, without sweeping hard questions under the carpet?
- What sorts of learning experiences can open up students' awareness of different perspectives and ways of knowing without giving the impression that anything goes?

We think that researchers and teachers will need to work together in tight partnerships as we all move further into the largely uncharted waters of capability development to address such questions. The complex futures that face our young people (and indeed us as citizens) are a reality. We all need to work together to prepare our young people to be active futures-makers, not just passive recipients of what fate may bring. The next two chapters further develop these ideas.

6
Working together to make a difference

Income gap widens faster in New Zealand

CONSUMERISM IS "EATING THE FUTURE"

Can You Buy Happiness?

ARE YOU PREPARED TO PAY
MORE TO SAVE THE PLANET?

Figure 6.1: News media headlines

Thinking about inequalities

NEW ZEALAND IS OFTEN described as being a place where everyone gets a fair go. Many New Zealanders consider our society to be less hierarchical than other countries and that people can quickly get their slice of the pie. But is this vision of New Zealand about the present, or the past? Like many countries in the "developed world", New Zealand now has a relatively high unemployment rate, low levels of employment security for some workers, increasing poverty, and a growing gap between rich and poor. The extent of this growing gap is starkly shown in the article in Box 6.1.

Income gap widens faster in New Zealand[1]

The gap between New Zealand's rich and poor has widened more than in any other developed country during the past 20 years, according to an OECD report.

Figures from the "Divided We Stand" think-tank show the income of the richest 10% of Kiwis is now more than 10 times that of the poorest 10% …

The OECD says the main driver behind rising income gaps has been greater inequality in wages and salaries, as the high-skilled have benefited more from technological progress than the low-skilled.

It warned about the rise of the high earners in rich societies and the falling share of income going to those at the bottom, saying governments must move quickly to tackle inequality.

"The social contract is starting to unravel in many countries," said OECD Secretary-General Angel Gurría in launching the report.

"This study dispels the assumptions that the benefits of economic growth will automatically trickle down to the disadvantaged and that greater inequality fosters greater social mobility. Without a comprehensive strategy for inclusive growth, inequality will continue to rise."

1. This is an excerpt. The full article can be found at: http://tvnz.co.nz/national-news/income-gap-widens-faster-in-new-zealand-4599042

Box 6.1: Income gap widens faster in New Zealand

> Gurría acknowledged reforms to boost competition and to make labour markets more adaptable, for example by promoting part-time work or more flexible hours, had promoted productivity and brought more people into work, especially women and low-paid workers.
>
> But the rise in part-time and low-paid work also extended the wage gap, the report said ...
>
> "There is nothing inevitable about high and growing inequalities," Gurría said.
>
> "Our report clearly indicates that upskilling of the workforce is by far the most powerful instrument to counter rising income inequality. The investment in people must begin in early childhood and be followed through into formal education and work ..."

Box 6.1 (*continued*)

The inequalities mentioned in Box 6.1 do not occur in isolation. They are connected to the global financial and economic instability we have been experiencing for some years. The causes of this instability, as well as the possible solutions, are multifaceted and complex (that is, it is a wicked problem). This instability is also interwoven with other wicked problems. One is a rise in consumerism. We now have more opportunities to buy cheap disposable stuff, and we get many messages about how purchasing more and more things will increase our wellbeing. This rise in consumerism is reinforcing inequality and poverty for some people. Unskilled jobs are being lost in Western countries, and people in developing countries are being used as dispensable workers who produce low-cost consumer goods, typically in poor working conditions. Their living conditions are also likely to be adversely impacted by environmental problems such as smog caused by mass manufacturing processes. A rise in consumerism is also associated with overuse of the world's natural resources, and is contributing to the pollution of the atmosphere as well as waterways and oceans. In these ways, overuse of resources has implications for climate change.

Making a difference to our world

Many people feel a sense of unease about the economic instability and consumerism our society is experiencing, and are taking action on a personal level to do something about it. Some have reacted by trying to simplify their lifestyle and reduce their carbon footprint. Young people are among those taking action. On TV and YouTube stories abound about young people who have been inspired from a personal experience to create change in their local or global community. But is it enough for each of us to act individually? Does there also need to be a focus on working collectively to create change? We think the answer to this question is "yes". This chapter starts from the premise that, to find and act on solutions to the wicked problems society faces, young people will need to work together to design solutions and then act on these. Some of the reasons why we think young people will need to work collectively are explained below.

In his TED talk[1] and book, *Prosperity without Growth: Economics for a Finite Planet*,[2] Tim Jackson argues that addressing instability by getting back on track with our current model of continuous economic growth is unsustainable for the planet. He says people need to think critically about this model and develop new joined-up scenarios which show that prosperity and wellbeing do not have to be linked to consumerism. What is needed are new ways of working which reduce our impact on the environment, and reduce inequality, but also promote economic stability. This rather complex and somewhat daunting task lies ahead for all of us—but particularly for our young people. To develop, evaluate, and enact solutions to the wicked problems society faces, young people will need to be able to cross current boundaries created by different disciplines such as economics, environmental science, and psychology.

---

1. For an overview of Tim Jackson's ideas about new economic models see his TED talk at: http://www.ted.com/talks/tim_jackson_s_economic_reality_check.html

2. In *Prosperity without Growth: Economics for a Finite Planet*, Jackson (2011) considers the complex relationships between economic growth, environmental crises, economic recession, and perceptions of wellbeing. He suggests that we need new models or ways to think about economic growth that are not based on the idea that both economic wellbeing and personal wellbeing are closely tied to a need to produce and consume an increasing number of material possessions. He offers some ideas about "green" economic models as one example of this new way of thinking.

They will need to participate and contribute in a range of communities, and work together to share ideas, world views, expertise, processes, and knowledge. They will also need the agency necessary to take action, even if each solution may not be the whole answer.

One implication of the challenge presented above is that schools will need to support young people to develop the knowledge, skills, values, and dispositions (that is, competencies) to work and act collectively. However, this idea of working together to create change poses two potential challenges to the current education system. One is creating space for students to develop their capacity to work with one another within a system that was founded on individual models of learning and assessment. The other is prioritising action, or learning by doing, in a system that has historically focused on "learning about" approaches to education.

Thinking about how to support young people to develop the capabilities they need to work collectively to take action is a central focus of this chapter. We broadly consider two questions: "What types of learning situations might provide young people with the agency and capabilities they need to work together to create change in society?" And, "What form do the key competencies need to take if one of their ultimate goals is to support change towards a better society?"

A successful life, or a decent life, or both?

By introducing the key competencies into the curriculum framework, the New Zealand education system has signalled a need to strengthen the focus on building young peoples' capabilities for living and lifelong learning. As we discussed at the start of this book, the OECD focus on a common set of competencies came from a desire to make sure that young people have the capabilities required to understand and deal with complex problems—such as the income disparities and inequality mentioned earlier. The OECD considers young people need to be able to address important social and economic challenges to have a "successful life" and contribute to a "well-functioning society".[3]

But who defines what is socially or economically important, or what a well-functioning society looks like? One debate in recent international literature about competencies stood out to us. The essence of this debate is that educational institutions are too focused on a market-driven view of competencies and how they might support a successful life through the development of vocational and employment skills.[4] As a result there is not enough emphasis on how competency development is linked to a well-functioning society. For example, is the main goal of university education to provide young people with the ability to get a "good" job and earn a high salary? Is it to support them to develop the capabilities needed to contribute to society?[5] Or is the goal to support young people to find a workable balance between these two areas, acknowledging that education is a public good as well as a private benefit?

Critics of market-driven interpretations suggest that the social-justice narrative underpinning competencies is not given enough priority. These critics argue that education systems need a greater focus on supporting young people to develop the capabilities needed for a "decent life" as active citizens who shape society for the good of all.[6] An emphasis on a decent life might increase the focus on human rights and social goals as an aspect of curriculum thinking. It also directs attention towards ideas about learning that focus on working together.

---

3. Background about the international development of the key competencies is covered in Chapter 1. For more details see *Key Competencies for a Successful Life and a Well-functioning Society*, edited by Rychen and Salganik (2003).
4. Hoskins (2008) and Lozano, Boni, Peris, and Hueso (2012) provide a critique of current competency frameworks and approaches in European countries.
5. For an example of this debate see the article by Pat Walsh who criticises a report which implies that the main goal of university education is a high income. See Walsh (2013), http://www.nzherald.co.nz/opinion/news/article.cfm?c_id=466&objectid=10864024
6. The idea of shifting the balance from a focus on a "successful life" to placing more emphasis on a "decent life" is suggested in Lozano et al. (2012). They discuss how a shift towards a decent life has implications for how we view learning and what is prioritised in classrooms.

> **NZC vision and principles**
> *Our vision is for young people*
> ... who will seize the opportunities offered by new knowledge and technologies to secure a sustainable social, cultural, economic, and environmental future for our country
> *Actively involved*
> Contributors to the well-being of New Zealand—social, cultural, economic, and environmental
> *Future focus*
> The curriculum encourages students to look to the future by exploring such significant future-focused issues such as sustainability, citizenship, enterprise, and globalisation.
> (Citizenship—exploring what it means to be a citizen and contribute to the development and well-being of society).

Box 6.2: *NZC vision and principles*

Messages in the curriculum about what's important

NZC can be interpreted as offering space to focus on a decent life. The vision statement, for example, balances economic and social goals (see Box 6.2).

NZC's principles also encourage schools to consider how the curriculum might enable students to contribute to society. For example, the principle that addresses big-picture future-focused issues includes exploration of what it means to be a citizen.

Statements in many of the learning areas also provide suggestions about how learning experiences could support young people to be active contributors to society. We'll introduce a few examples later in this chapter.

The extent to which a view of students as active contributors could drive a school's curriculum depends on the big-picture vision of the school, and what this vision looks like when it is put into action. Whether more space is created for students to be active contributors will depend on how the vision, values, key competencies, and the learning areas in *NZC* are woven together, and the nature of the learning experiences that follow from this design process.

If we agree that promoting a decent life is an important priority, and that *NZC* gives us ample space to do this, the next question we need to ask is, "Are certain types of learning experiences or contexts for learning more likely than others to support young people to be contributors to society?"

A decent life: Enabling students to work collectively

We all hear many messages from different sources about the need to transform education so that it develops young people who are equipped for the demands of the 21st century. Some writers suggest that, to support young people to take a more active role in their world, educators and policy makers need to reconsider the emphasis placed on individual and competitive approaches to learning. One suggestion is that education systems need to increase their focus on promoting a stronger sense of collectivity and a larger view of the world.[7] One way of promoting collectivity is to create space for students to work together to design and engage in actions that address meaningful problems.[8] This

---

7. For example, see Johnson and Morris (2010) who summarise what an "ideal" critical citizenship education might look like in schools. They offer a framework with four key dimensions. One dimension is an emphasis on the social or a sense of collectivity, which incorporates the ability to interact and work with others in ways that show awareness of non-dominant perspectives. A second dimension is engagement or praxis, which incorporates ideas about imagining a better world, knowledge of social change processes, and taking collective action towards new visions. The other two dimensions are politics (e.g., knowledge of power structures, skills in social analysis) and self (e.g., sense of identity, knowledge of your own position). Johnson and Morris's model explores the different sets of knowledge, skills, values, and dispositions young people might need to develop in relation to each of the four dimensions.
8. See Apple and Beane (2007) for a discussion about the need for approaches to learning that enable young people to critique their current world and work together to solve real problems. Apple and Beane's approach is underpinned by critical pedagogy as developed by writers and social activists such as Michael Apple, as well as Paulo Freire (1993). Critical pedagogy emphasises dialogue and working with others, and makes a strong connection between thinking and doing—which is termed "praxis" (bringing together critical reflection and action in ways that challenge the structures which disadvantage some groups). Apple and Beane's work also draws on Dewey's ideas about how schools can promote citizenship through enabling young people to learn by actively and collaboratively tackling real-life problems (for example, see Dewey, 1916).

makes intuitive sense—many of us like to feel we can work together to make a real difference.

A collective and action-orientated approach to learning stands in contrast to approaches which prioritise learning about knowledge generated by others. A traditional approach typically takes the form of students working by themselves (often as part of an inquiry project) to summarise information as a report, poster, or assignment. Students are not necessarily asked to do something new with this information.[9] We have seen in many schools that the taking-action step of a student inquiry cycle (Figure 6.2) can be downplayed or ignored. The core learning is seen to be located within the inquiry steps that emphasise the formation of questions and the gathering and interpreting of information.

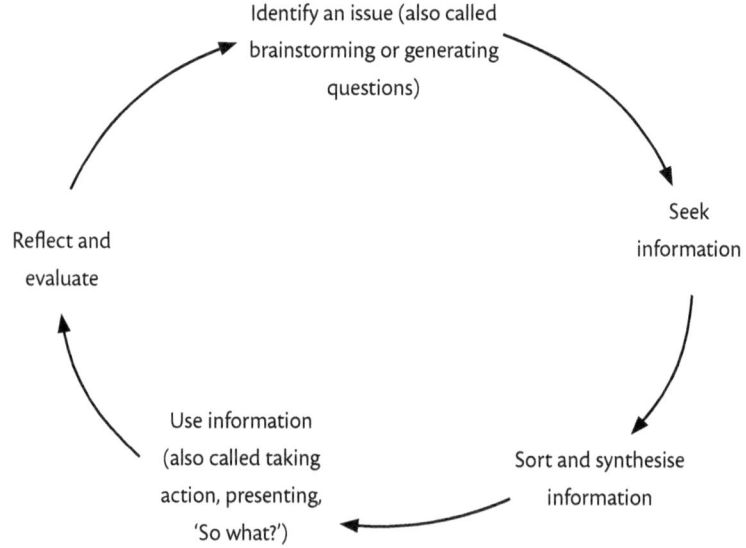

Figure 6.2: A generic student inquiry cycle

---

9. For a discussion about why is it important to think about knowledge as something that students can "do things with" as opposed to being "stuff" that is developed by experts and summarised as facts by students, see Gilbert (2005), *Catching the Knowledge Wave?*.

Increasing the focus on collective actions that promote a decent life has implications for how learning experiences are designed and how key competencies are understood. Questions such as this come to the fore: what are the dispositions and capabilities young people might need to create social change and transformation within a group? To work towards a successful life, individuals need to feel they have the agency to create this life for themselves. However, if a decent life is also a key end goal, then agency is an important platform from which individuals can engage in collective action and participate in society.[10]

In Box 6.3 we present two examples of approaches which give students agency to participate and contribute to collective actions.

Example 1

Supporting wellbeing in a "happy, clean, friendly, and long lasting school"

This school[1] has a history of environmental education which started in 2003 when a group of parents developed a permaculture garden. By 2008, the school had an enviro-club which included a large number of students from different year levels. The club was supported by a lead teacher, a parent, and a facilitator from the Enviroschools programme. Being part of the enviro-club offered students a wide range of leadership opportunities. Students managed the school recycling bins, litter collection, vegetable garden, and worm farm, and provided healthy vege soup lunches for their peers. To encourage new club members, students educated younger students about recycling. They also ran

---

1. This description was part of series of case studies that aimed to explore school approaches to health and wellbeing connected to the Fruit in Schools initiative. This adapted excerpt focuses on the activities of a school's enviro-club. For the full case study see Boyd and Moss (2009).

Box 6.3: Two examples of approaches which give students agency to participate and contribute to collective actions—the enviro-club and the Youth Health Council

---

10. See Lozano et al. (2012) and Sen (1999) cited in Lozano et al., for a discussion about why it is important to consider concepts such as agency from a holistic and collective, as well as individual, perspective.

consultation processes with their peers as they worked to improve the way the school promoted healthy lifestyles and wellbeing.

In 2008, the enviro-club was in the middle of a consultation and visioning process to develop new priorities. This process was being supported by an Enviroschools facilitator. Students' new vision for the school was to be "happy, clean, friendly, and long lasting".

Through the consultation process students were starting to develop priorities for the next year that reflected their vision of wellbeing for people and the environment, and which balanced different interests. Examples included: improving the hall so students could practise and perform plays and cultural group activities; the planting of fruit trees; and marking the field for sports practices. To get input from others, students drew a map of the school to show the location of possible priorities. The map was located in the library, and other students and teachers were invited to put stickies on to add their comments and ideas.

Curriculum links

Teachers considered the school's enviro-activities were more effective when they had a curriculum focus. Many activities were linked to the curriculum programme (e.g., integrated units on water and recycling; classroom activities that contributed to a local community expo on energy saving; and technology projects that resulted in some students designing and building a water collector for the garden, which did not have a nearby water supply).

Community connections

Over time the enviro-club had made many connections with the wider community. They linked with the local playcentre to share a water supply and assist in the development of the playcentre garden. As well as connections with a local Enviroschool facilitator and the regional Sustainability Trust, the school had links with the local city council which has a zero waste education programme for schools. Staff and students attended the council's courses on organic gardening

Box 6.3 *(continued)*

and worm farming, which contributed to the school's focus on recycling.

By 2013 the school had developed their approach to make the garden more integral to the curriculum programme, owned by all students, and sustainable in the longer term. Students from each syndicate team now have responsibility for parts of the garden. Recently, each team took turns to see how they could use vegetables from the garden to produce healthy low-cost lunches for their peers.

Example 2

Projects designed for impact

Supporting the process through planning and portfolios

Before a project begins,[2] students present a project proposal to teachers for feedback and refinement. Students outline how their project will link to the four principles that underpin successful impact projects. These are:

1. student ownership and commitment to the project topic
2. quality outcomes including a product
3. substantial learning beyond the classroom
4. the project enables students to participate and contribute with their community.

As students work to progress their project, they use a portfolio to document their plan, timelines, and team-member roles; the activities they have completed and evidence of learning; their reflections; and the criteria they will use to judge whether the process they designed was successful. These criteria are often developed and refined throughout the course of the project in consultation with their teacher and other experts.

---

2. This description is of a project undertaken by two Year 12 students. They attend a school that supports students to complete individual or collective projects relating to their interests and passions. There is an expectation that projects will be meaningful for the wider community and that students will work with community stakeholders. The projects are often cross-curricula and students conceptualise and design their projects using an inquiry cycle that links to project-based learning approaches. The school has impact project days once a week. For more information about impact projects see http://www.ashs.school.nz/curriculum/impact-projects

Box 6.3 (*continued*)

Student project statement: Youth Health Council

Our impact project[3] is about raising awareness of mental health issues that teenagers face by developing a Youth Health Council to address these mental health issues. With help from Youthline, who are a major stakeholder in our project, we aim to create a successful and sustaining Youth Health Council which will create and run events to bring the awareness that mental health issues need, such as anxiety and depression. Along the way we are gaining knowledge about different mental illnesses and creating resources, such as videos, for others to use as a learning source.

This project is continued from our previous project which involved creating a website exploring the idea of change from a mental health point of view (see http://www.inspired-by-change.com). As part of this project we completed the Health Standard 91097 1.3: Demonstrate understanding of ways in which wellbeing can change and strategies to support wellbeing.

This first project gave us good groundwork to start the second project because it helped us establish a relationship with Youthline and other organizations such as Rainbow Youth and also gave us another resource which we could use.

For this project, students note the following success criteria:

- Expand our personal knowledge on mental health and apply our current knowledge (from the last project) by focusing on depression and anxiety.
- Develop a survey for students about mental health issues to collect valid and accurate data about what health issues students face that we could help with in some way.
- Use this data to create at least one event or project that raises awareness about or helps with, a health issue found from our data. (Current plans are to lead an assembly for Year 11s with a presentation on depression and self esteem which will also promote the Youth Health Council.)
- Make the Youth Health Council known throughout the school and get more students on board in order to create and maintain a strong council that

---

3. This description is adapted from the students' project statement and portfolio entries.

Box 6.3 (*continued*)

> *continues in coming years.*
>
> *Setting learning and key-competency-related goals*
>
> Students set individual and group goals in their portfolio. Some of these goals are about building aspects of the key competencies. For this project, examples of goals include:
> - Group goals: *We will develop personal knowledge and understanding about mental health and current issues teens are facing. This will continue on from our previous project and the learning will benefit us in our specialist subject health, as well as gaining a better understanding about possible career paths in this field.*
> - Individual goals: *I will be successful if I can develop my leadership skills through:*
>   1. *Speaking in front of groups of students, teachers and organisations e.g. board of trustees, Youthline, Impact community.*
>   2. *Taking new students on board as the project develops and being a good leader of the Youth Health Council.*
>   3. *Developing other skills to help with leadership e.g., time management, staying on task, organisation etc.*

Box 6.3 *(continued)*

Taking critical and collective action: Bringing the key competencies together

At the heart of the examples given in Box 6.3 is a desire by the two schools to create opportunities for students to *participate and contribute* to create real change in their school community. Working collectively to take action requires students to draw on aspects of more than one key competency. The boundaries between each key competency are overlapped. Having a clear sense of what is in and what is out for these boundaries is less important than being clear about the main capabilities that are being fostered through a learning situation, why these are a focus, and how scaffolding and support will be provided to students.

Working with a team of peers

In the enviro-club and Youth Health Council examples given in Box 6.3, students were supported to use health promotion processes and activities[11] (for example, needs analysis, visioning, consultation and community empowerment, priority setting, planning and action, reflecting and evaluating). Health promotion requires students to use their knowledge and weave it with their team members' ideas and input from wider community consultations. The ultimate aim is to create new ways of promoting health and wellbeing that involve and suit the people in a particular setting. To effectively design new ways to promote health and wellbeing, students need to form, and work with, a range of communities. The students at both schools were part of a small core team who worked together to decide on and design new approaches for their school.

Over a number of years, as we have visited schools to talk to students, they have often mentioned their struggles with group work and how they are not really sure of its purpose or how to manage their peers. Supporting students to work effectively as team members and leaders is likely to require facilitation by teachers, as well as scaffolding, as students learn new ways to be in a group. Working with others requires students to draw on a range of aspects of *relating to others*, including active listening, sharing ideas, and working together to develop new ideas. One key starting point for working together is being able to empathise with others and have a sense that a collective might build knowledge in different ways from individuals. We have expanded on these ideas in Chapter 3.

---

11. Health promotion is one of four interrelated core concepts in the Health and Physical Education learning area in *NZC*. The World Health Organization defines health promotion as "the process of enabling people to increase control over, and to improve, their health." See http://www.who.int/healthpromotion/conferences/previous/ottawa/en/index.html. For more information about the range of activities that come under the wider umbrella of health promotion see http://www.who.int/healthpromotion/conferences/previous/ottawa/en/index1.html

Creating and belonging to communities
Working in a group with peers connects to the dimensions of the key competency *participating and contributing* that are about being actively involved and developing a sense of belonging. *Participating and contributing* is also about making connections with new communities (in and outside school) and creating space for their contributions. Creating space for others is not just about letting others talk. It can require students to put aside their own plans and acknowledge that others might contribute ideas that are more likely to achieve the group's aim. For this to happen, students will have to learn about when to lead, and when to let others take this role.

In the enviro-club and Youth Health Council examples, the student teams experienced first-hand some of the strategies that can be used to hear and consider different perspectives, and balance the needs and wishes of different groups. The students in the enviro-club designed a process that involved students and staff contributing their ideas onto a map of the school. Enviro-club students then considered the interests of their peers and selected a range of ideas to implement which attempted to fairly balance different interests. The students also formed new communities with people outside school. With assistance from adults, the enviro-club students formed connections with people outside the school who could give them expert advice. The students in the Youth Health Council example did the same. As older students, they were able to make or maintain new connections and build relationships with external groups themselves.

Thinking about values and ethics
Each community or group may have a different perspective or values position on an issue. These differences determine the actions they might take in regard to that issue. To balance the needs and perspectives of different groups, young people will need to learn how different values positions underlie different actions, and develop their ability to

think ethically and fairly.[12] An understanding of different positions is particularly important when considering solutions to complex problems, as there is no one right answer, and some solutions may disadvantage some groups. Ethical thinking is about building awareness of social-justice concerns and weighing up the implications of different solutions, considering whose interests are being served, and endeavouring to find solutions that consider the needs of possibly disadvantaged groups. Developing their ability to think ethically could also support young people to maintain an individual identity within the collective so they can avoid any possibility of brainwashing or "group think" that can occur in groups.[13]

Thinking critically and creatively about the wider system

For students in the enviro-club and the Youth Health Council, the creation of a new vision or priorities for the future made them think critically about the way their school currently promoted health and wellbeing, either for people or the environment, and what could be improved. Critical thinking is a starting point for reviewing how our immediate community or society promotes a decent life. This could involve challenging views or practices that are currently taken for granted. One way of creating a space to think about things we take for granted is through learning experiences that make the familiar strange. This is an idea we'll come back to in the next chapter.

The vision and priorities that the enviro-club students were developing also called for creative thinking. These priorities reflected students' desire to support the health and wellbeing of people, and use local resources in a sustainable fashion. For example, the planting of fruit trees was part of

---

12. For ideas about how to explore ethical decision-making and judgements with students in science contexts see: http://www.sciencelearn.org.nz/Thinking-Tools/Ethics-thinking-tool

13. Johnson and Morris (2010) outline the benefits and challenges of developing a sense of collectivity. One challenge is avoiding "group think", which refers to the situation in which an individual's desire to create consensus overrides their ability to speak up even if they consider group actions are not likely to be effective or could have damaging impacts. A related challenge, which is called "mob mentality", is also discussed in Davis, Sumara, and Luce-Kapler (2000)—where people instinctively follow others which results in actions that might be detrimental to themselves or (Hines & Bishop, 2006) others, rather than trusting their own judgement.

a long-term plan that had at least four different aims. These included a Sunsmart (sun protection) focus on providing shelter from the sun and wind at break-times; providing fruit to support the healthy-eating focus at the school that was one way of addressing concerns about food security for low-income families; and enhancing the school grounds whilst also supporting a local tree-planting programme. In combination, these aims were about promoting the wellbeing of people in ways that also promoted the wellbeing of the environment. Encouraging students to think about the joined-up nature of these aims could be an opportunity for teachers to introduce some of the systems-thinking ideas discussed in Chapter 4.

Individual and collective agency
In the enviro-club and Youth Health Council examples, working through actions gave students a sense of individual and collective agency. The students saw themselves as people who were making a meaningful difference to their immediate world. Enviro-club students had gained a strong sense of empowerment and collective pride in being members of their group. They told us how important it was for them to do something "real". Their school activities also built or enhanced the passions and interests they were pursuing outside school. The Youth Health Council students were building on the confidence and capabilities they developed through an earlier project to look outwards and involve a broader range of people and groups in creating change.

Working through ups and downs is an inevitable part of shared projects. Navigating a path through roadblocks requires confidence, a can-do attitude, persistence, and leadership. The schools which enabled the enviro-club and Youth Health Council projects both provided scaffolding in the form of clearly defined processes for students to work through. This teacher or adult support was appropriate to the age and stage of students. These collective projects were about giving students more space to take a lead. This meant that a more open-ended curriculum-planning process and longer time frames were also needed.

The learning area challenge: Connecting collective critical action with the learning areas

In our experience, activities that come under the umbrella of collective actions often sit on the fringe of formal curriculum planning as optional or extracurricular activities. This position on the fringe suggests that curriculum planning is driven by the idea that school learning is mostly about preparing students for a future role as active citizens. In this framing, being prepared means learning about how society works, so students will be ready to use the knowledge they gain at some stage in the future. Offering young people opportunities to engage in collective actions shifts this frame. As they work to make a difference to their world these students are active citizens now—they do not need to wait for the future.[14]

NZC's learning areas, or aspects of learning areas, offer many spaces for students to participate as active citizens who create change. As they work collectively, students demonstrate and develop the key competencies by drawing on knowledge as well as skills, values, and dispositions. The enviro-club and Youth Health Council examples in this chapter draw on content knowledge and processes related to the Healthy Communities and Environments strand of the Health and Physical Education learning area. The enviro-club is also linked to education for sustainability and environmental education.[15] A focus on sustainability provides opportunities to work across a number of learning areas. Other individual learning areas, such as Social Sciences or Arts, also provide a space for students to work together in ways that challenge viewpoints while also building a sense of citizenship and community wellbeing. This is by no means an exhaustive list. These sorts of opportunities can be created in all learning areas.

We also need to think about working across learning area boundaries.

---

14. For more information about these different ways of thinking about the role of learners (learners as active citizens or learners in preparation) see Boyd and Hipkins (2012) and Boyd (2013).
15. Sustainability is named in *NZC* as one example of a future-focused issue. Future-focused issues are cross-cutting themes. Learning experiences that relate to these themes are likely to encourage rich learning opportunities as they tend to require students to make connections across learning areas in ways that also link with the values and key competencies in the curriculum.

Wicked problems have multiple and interrelated causes, impacts, and solutions which span many learning areas. Therefore, students are likely to benefit from learning in situations which enable them to consider a range of causes and impacts, and work towards solutions that draw on the processes and knowledge sets found in the different learning areas.[16]

Students as active citizens: Competencies for now and the future
In this chapter we have explored some of the dimensions of collective critical action. *NZC* offers space to design collective learning experiences that promote change—if we choose to read the curriculum that way. Currently, the priority given to students engaging in collective actions varies. It is likely that this variation reflects different views about learners as well as the purpose of education (that is, are students citizens in preparation or active citizens now?)

This book is about key competencies for the future. *NZC* tells us that learning experiences need to enable young people to promote the social, cultural, economic, and environmental wellbeing of New Zealand. Making a sense of collectivism an integral part of curriculum, pedagogy, and assessment practices is one way of broadening views about the range of learning experiences that might build the capabilities needed to create change. Through our work in schools we are seeing a growing number of students who are engaged in thoughtful and empowering collective actions that aim to make their immediate world a better place. We have talked to many students whose eyes light up as they describe their experiences of doing something that is real. These activities often give students a strong sense of belonging to their school and wider communities. They can be the hook that re-engages students who are bored with school. However, these collective actions often sit on the fringes of the curriculum programme. Our hope is that New Zealand teachers can build on these examples so they can become a core part of

---
16. For examples of approaches that integrate across learning areas in New Zealand primary schools see Fraser, Aitken, and Whyte (2013). For secondary school examples from an international setting see Apple and Beane (2007).

curriculum learning. Then, collectively, we will all increase our focus on *participating and contributing* to a decent life for all.

7

Key competencies for future-building educators

School quick to embrace the future

"INFORMED, THOUGHTFUL CITIZENS"
AT RISK OF VANISHING: ACADEMICS

**SCHOOLS STRUGGLE
AS MORE STUDENTS SEEK HELP**

The education debacle:
How do we solve this problem?

Figure 7.1: News media headlines

Rethinking the future of learning

We are nearing the end of our book. We know we have covered a lot of challenging ground, tackling complex and politically charged issues, such as climate change, food security, social and economic inequalities, and what it means to aspire to a decent life for all. While these issues may not be the usual fodder for school conversations about key competencies, there is a reason we grabbed controversial stories from the headlines as we pieced this book together. If education is to be a relevant tool for helping people to live a decent life in the world we have, and, more importantly, enable us to shape the world we aspire to live in, we think schools ought to be engaging with these kinds of issues to generate opportunities for learning.

Throughout the book we have tried to maintain a consistent focus on "key competencies for the future" by providing a line of sight between learning activities that can help develop school learners' competencies now, and some of the long-term challenges to which learners may need to apply those capabilities. We've woven in stories from practice, and shared our own ideas and questions about how schools might better support the development of young people who are confident and capable of tackling a wide range of wicked problems. However, this book is not a how-to guide. If you are a teacher or school leader, we hope the ideas and examples we offer will help you to reflect on possibilities for practice in your own schools. If you're a parent, a student, or anyone else with an interest in education, we hope this book will help you to have richer conversations about the future of learning and find ways actively to support and encourage those who are trying to help make it happen.

Speaking of *you*, in this chapter we're shifting the focus from students' competencies to your competencies for the future (and ours as well). We'll look at some of the questions we face as people who want to support deep, transformative, competency-building learning for students. What competencies or capabilities do we all need in order to provide the conditions for these kinds of learning? And what are our responsibilities for helping to transform the wider structures and systems that shape, support, and enable those conditions for learning? These questions rise to the surface as we address the wicked problem closest to home: the challenge of how we might reimagine and reorient ourselves, and our educational systems and structures, for a better future.

Can our education systems be transformed?
Let's start by taking a closer look at this wicked problem. Educational theorists have long argued that current schooling approaches are not sufficient to address and support 21st-century learning needs.[1] The internet is abuzz with videos, podcasts, blogs, and no shortage of opinions about what 21st-century education ought to be—or ought not to be.[2] All this talk implies some degree of consensus that changes are needed, but what exactly needs to change, and how? Here, perspectives vary. And no wonder: while the public sphere contains plenty of calls for transformative changes in the way we do education, there are even more widely accepted ideas and beliefs which reinforce existing practices, systems, and structures that may not be as relevant or fit-for-purpose as they once were. Can we, collectively, really help our educational system to change in courageous and genuinely future-focused directions? Are big shifts needed, or should we just tinker around at the edges, trying incrementally to improve what we are doing in small ways here and there?

We do think small steps count. But to make a big difference, they have to be connected with big thinking about where we're going. To achieve genuinely transformative changes, one prominent educational commentator from the United Kingdom suggests that "a new consensus needs to be forged about the kind of learning we should aspire to provide",[3] a consensus that parents, children, teachers, and policy makers can all buy into. If we all work on this wicked problem together, perhaps we might actually be able to build something more suited to achieving a better future. But what exactly is this "better"? Better for whom, or

---
1. See, for example, Gilbert (2005), Egan (2008), Kress (2008), and Leadbeater (2011).
2. TED talks such as Sir Ken Robinson's widely shared "How schools kill creativity" lecture are illustrative.
3. Leadbeater (2011), p. 6.

for what? And how do we do it together? Is it about building new or different kinds of schools? Changing the curriculum? Developing more effective ways of defining and assessing learning? Thinking differently about teachers' professional learning and development? Getting more technology in schools? What about de-schooling[4] altogether? Like any good wicked problem, there are as many different answers as there are different ways to frame the problem. Where could we start?

Future building, not future proofing
To an extent, we think it works to start anywhere, as long as wherever we start, we examine ideas about the future and talk about the purposes of education for the future. Keri Facer captured our imagination with her call for schools and the wider community to see their responsibilities not in terms of future proofing, but in terms of future building.[5] Future proofing conveys a sense of planning ahead to stave off the potentially negative consequences of a knowable or perhaps inevitable future (much as we might weatherproof our homes against storms). However, the notion of future building[6] tells a slightly different story. Here, the future isn't cast as something that is simply going to happen to us, but as something that we are going to make happen. Of course, future proofing and future building do leave room for the future to be predictable (to an extent) and unpredictable (to an extent). The difference is that future building implies we have power and agency to create the future we want. As Facer points out, this isn't about having "stupid optimism" that everything will turn out for the best. Nor can we realistically assume that absolutely any future we can hope for is possible, because some

---

4. Here's a definition copied from Wikipedia: "Deschooling is a term used by both education philosophers and proponents of alternative education and/or homeschooling, though it refers to different things in each context. It was popularized by Ivan Illich in his 1971 book *Deschooling Society.*"
5. Keri Facer expresses these ideas clearly in her 2011 book *Learning Futures: Education, Technology and Social Change*. We also recommend this 15-minute video http://www.youtube.com/watch?v=D_EcMTRKt8k
6. Some people dislike the "building" or "constructing" metaphor that is often used in eduspeak. We don't have a problem with these terms, but if you do, you might prefer to think about alternative metaphors that work for you. Painting or sculpting the future, imagining and realising the future, growing the future, and so forth.

futures are far more probable than others. Professional futurists are good at rigorously analysing and forecasting what *could* happen, but any futurists worth their salt will quickly dispel the notion that they can predict the future with any certainty. Instead, they will urge you to understand the twofold purposes of forecasting possible futures. First, future forecasting helps to identify what could happen (moving from infinite possible futures to various probable futures as we forecast and reforecast with the knowledge we currently have).[7] Secondly, forecasting what might happen can clarify what we actually *want* to happen from the range of plausible possibilities. Carefully visioning a desired future helps us (in theory at least) to reorganise what we are doing now to maximise our chances of achieving it.[8]

Key competencies for future-building educators

What individual and collective capabilities do we need to call on both to identify the future we want and to plan towards it? The idea of achieving at least some greater degree of consensus about the future of learning suggests we need better opportunities for everyone in the system—from teachers and learners through to families and whānau, communities, educational policy leaders, and other influential people—to actively discuss their ideas, expectations, experiences, and aspirations for education and the future. This brings up a capability already discussed in Chapter 3: the ability to work with diverse others and ideas. There, we saw that working with diverse people and ideas is challenging because it is value-laden, and often requires people to adapt or change their views, or sometimes let go of certain ideas or conditions which have historically been to their advantage. The capabilities and capability-building learning opportunities described in Chapter 3 for learners are also very relevant for future-building educators. We all need to be able

---

7. For more about future forecasting we recommend these books *Thinking About the Future* (Hines & Bishop, 2006) and *Teaching About the Future* (Bishop & Hines, 2012).
8. Future-studies professional Dr Peter Bishop notes that the first purpose of future studies is to *understand change* in order to be able to start to describe expected and other plausible future states. The second purpose, *influencing change* means to bring about the best possible future for ourselves and others, given the time and resources we have available (Bishop, 2005).

to talk each other's talk, stand in the shoes of others, and so on. We also need the capabilities to help other people do these things.

Being a future-building educator also requires deep thought. But what kinds of thinking are needed? Forecasting alternative futures requires careful analytical thinking, but it also requires imaginative thinking. Many people and organisations have used systematic analytical forecasting and imaginative processes to develop different possible scenarios for the future of schooling.[9] There are also good books and materials that help to kick off these types of thinking processes.[10] For now, we're going to look at a creative realm in which alternative futures are routinely imagined and described in great detail: science fiction. (We'll return to the educational futures literature later.)

Why science fiction?
Our purpose in looking at science fiction is not to seek ideas about how the future ought to be, but rather to illustrate some of the interesting things that happen when human minds think about the future. Try it for a few moments. Close your eyes and imagine waking up on a Tuesday morning 30 years in the future. What comes to mind? Where are you? Who are you? What do you see and hear? What are things like? What's familiar and what's different?

What futurists, science-fiction writers, advertisers, and artists know is that people's visions of the future tend to conjure an eclectic mixture of different imagery, ideas, and feelings. What's more, all of us tend to fluidly switch between different imagery and feelings, with some parts of our lives governed by one set of ideas about the future (let's say, that the future is going to be better) and other parts of our lives governed by another set of ideas (let's say, the gnawing anxiety that we are spiralling

---

9. These include UNESCO's International Commission on Education for the Twenty-first Century (see Delors, 1996, 1998), the OECD DeSeCo project (e.g., Rychen & Salganik, 2003), New Zealand's Secondary Futures project, a similar UK-based project called Educational Futures (edfuturesresearch.org), and many others. See also Bolstad et al., (2012).
10. In addition to the sources already footnoted, we recommend spending some time browsing on Metafuture http://www.metafuture.org/ and Design Thinking for Educators http://designthinkingforeducators.com/

towards environmental or social collapse).[11] Most of us, most of the time, are quietly going about our daily lives and flip-flopping between a lot of different ideas about the future—and why not? The future is unwritten. We'll eventually find out how things play out when it becomes the present. Do we need to pay much attention to whether our imaginings are useful, accurate, consistent, or otherwise? Here, we need to anchor ourselves against passively drifting into the future—if our imaginations are part of what helps us to create and work towards a future we actually want, then how we imagine different possible futures does matter.

Science fiction provides us with one way into an imagining process. Science-fiction writers have a great deal of freedom to imagine worlds beyond the plausibility constraints of the present. What makes science fiction compelling is that writers don't just imagine one little piece of the future. They imagine a whole world or system of worlds, and populate it with characters through whose eyes we inhabit and experience that system and the relationships within it. Thus we come to see in quite a deep way how different elements of that imagined system interact— how that future society is structured, the politics, technologies, beliefs, and practices of the beings that inhabit that system, the relationships between the biological and the technological, and so on. And of course, as art imitates life and vice versa, science fiction (or fiction, or art of any kind) also helps us recognise certain aspects of our present beliefs, habits, and conditions. Teasing these ideas out through fiction sometimes makes them easier for us to critique, and perhaps to resist.[12]

For the future of education, this is where it gets interesting. It's surprising how often science-fiction authors present us with radically different social and technological future worlds, yet within these we find quite conventional and even stereotyped representations of schools

---

11. We picked up this notion from Future Studies Professor James Dator, who argues that all images of the future can be collapsed into four main categories that he calls continued growth, collapse, disciplined society, and transformation. His ideas are provocative and accessible. You can read more in Dator (In press), "Four images of the future", or in his video address on the New Zealand Futures Trust website http://www.futurestrust.org.nz/

12. For another take on science fiction and future education, see Andrew Gibbons' (In press) article "Ah the serenity… Absurd ideas about educational futures" in the Future Education special issue of set: Research Information for Teachers.

and teaching. Let's look at two examples: *Ender's Game,* by Orson Scott Card, and *The Diamond Age,* by Neal Stephenson. We know there are probably other science-fiction stories which offer more creative and inspiring notions of schools and learning in the future. Perhaps you have read or seen some interesting ones yourself.[13] But we've chosen these two novels to open up some provocative questions you can apply to your own futures thinking.

Ender's Game
Learning at desks, or learning without gravity?
Ender's Game is a 1985 novel popular with school-age readers (and recently a 2013 feature film). It is set in a fictional future in which humans travel in space and are at war with an alien race of giant insects. Earth is ruled by a military organisation, The International Fleet, which uses implanted devices to monitor the children of Earth to search for those with special gifts and aptitudes. One of these children is a young boy named Ender Wiggin. Look at how his school classroom is described at the beginning of the book.

> The bell rang. Everyone signed off their desks or hurriedly typed reminders to themselves. Some were dumping lessons or data into their computers at home ... Ender spread his hands over the child-size keyboard near the edge of the desk and wondered what it would feel like to have hands as large as a grown-up's. They must feel so big and awkward, thick stubby fingers and beefy palms. Of course, they had bigger keyboards—but how could their thick fingers draw a fine line, the way Ender could. A line so precise that he could make it spiral seventy-nine times from the center to the edge without the lines every touching or overlapping. It gave him something to do while the teacher droned on about arithmetic. (Card, 1985, pp. 5–6)

Box 7.1: *Ender's Game*: Learning at desks, or learning without gravity?

---

13. If you have some good examples, please email rachel.bolstad@nzcer.org.nz or post a note on www.facebook.com/ShiftingThinkingNZCER

The imagery above doesn't paint a particularly inspiring vision of school in the future (making matters worse, in the next few paragraphs Ender is attacked after class by a group of school bullies). Reading on we discover that it's only by leaving this school behind that Ender's real learning journey begins. The next day, Ender is plucked from this school (and, probably to his relief, from the droning mathematics teacher) and sent to a very different kind of learning institution: the elite Battle School in Earth's orbit. The Battle School itself draws on another conventional formula for a school: a military academy built on regimented order and "drop and give me twenty" discipline. However, what's interesting is the way that Ender and the other child cadets learn in this school, specifically in The Battle Room, an immersive and game-like combat simulation where the students fly around in zero gravity in a three-dimensional space. The Battle Room, and Ender's rise to become a complex, thoughtful, moral leader whose actions on the world end up transforming it, are the real centrepiece of the story.

The author of *Ender's Game*, Orson Scott Card, explained that the idea for the Battle Room was sparked by reading stories of pilots training for aerial combat in the World War One, and the challenges they faced in having to learn to think quickly in three dimensions:

> I had read ... that it was very hard at first for pilots in WWI to learn to look above them and below them rather than merely to the left and right, to find the enemy approaching them in the air. *How much worse, then, would it be to learn to think with no up and down at all*? (Card, 1985, p. xii, italics added)

This compelling thought triggered his imagination—how could space commanders learn to think differently about movement in space, where the old idea of up and down simply don't apply? The Battle Room began to form in his mind. Only years later did he fully develop a storyline and characters to wrap around it, and *Ender's Game* was born.

Box 7.1 (*continued*)

Orson Scott Card dreamt up a whole novel from the idea of learning to think without gravity through a completely immersive bodily game-like learning experience. Yet he presented us with a very flat view of ordinary Earth school, with a droning teacher, students at desks, and a disengaging curriculum. Why? You might have noticed the publication date for *Ender's Game*, and further deduced that the Earth classroom Card describes perhaps sounds a bit like a classroom from 1985, and the Battle Room feels like the kind of computer-game-learning environment that a bored schoolchild in 1985 might well have fantasised about.[14] The author himself tends to emphasise the book as a story that asserts children's personhood—even as "a perpetual, self-renewing underclass, helpless to escape from the decisions of adults until they become adults themselves" (Card, 1885, p. xx). *Ender's Game* can also be read as a political critique of the Cold War, along with many other interpretations. All of these readings underscore the fact that science-fiction systems of the future are products of their time and context as much as they are of their authors' imaginations. They are also a product of deliberate choices that the author makes for the story he or she wants to tell. These are all important ideas to carry with us as we get closer to doing our own educational futures thinking. We'll get to that, but in Box 7.2 we have another book to consider: *The Diamond Age*, by Neal Stephenson.

‿

---

14. While some educational games are used in schools and classrooms, research and development around the deep learning potential, impacts, and contexts of use for immersive games and simulations in mainstream educational research, curriculum and assessment design, and classroom practice has, in our opinion, been surprisingly limited. Squire (2006) contends that game environments are built on a grammar of "being and doing", in contrast to the more familiar notions of school learning as transmission and absorption of knowledge. Promisingly, there have been recent turns in the game development industry towards Serious Games (Michael & Chen, 2005) which have an explicit and carefully designed educational purpose, and the notion of gamification—the use of game thinking and game mechanics in non-game contexts to engage users in solving problems (see Gee, 2003, and Squire, 2011).

The Diamond Age
Nanotechnology and disciplined children

The Diamond Age by Neal Stephenson is a 1995 cyberpunk novel which tells of a future that is infused with nanotechnology, within a highly socially stratified and globalised society. Nation-states have disappeared, and instead people are spread around the world belonging to "phyles" or tribes with different values which coexist with common economic trade protocols. One such phyle is the Neo-Victorians, a high-tech group who have adopted some of the social values and habits of the 19th century, preferring these "stable social models" over the social habits of more recent centuries, in which they found "little ... worthy of emulation" (p. 24). In the world of *The Diamond Age*, "nanotechnology had made nearly anything possible" (p. 37). Yet amidst all of this we once again see traditional stereotyped images of schooling projected into the future, such as "ranks of uniformed schoolchildren" (p. 7) subjected to classroom approaches that one character describes as "an ordeal she had to sit through in order to experience the fun parts of the curriculum" (p. 316). The Neo-Victorian's penchant for 19th-century English tradition extends to corporal punishment and, for particularly unruly students, the euphemistically named Saturday morning "supplementary curriculum" class.

> Each Saturday, Nell, Fiona, and Elizabeth would arrive at the school at seven o'clock, enter the room, and sit down in the front row in adjacent desks ... There was no teacher in the room at any time. They assumed that they were being monitored, but they never really knew. When they entered, each one of them had a pile of books on her desk—old books bound in chafed leather. Their job was to copy the books out by hand and leave the pages neatly stacked on Miss Stricken's desk before they went home. (p. 317)

The narrative in *The Diamond Age* makes it very clear these ways of schooling children are nothing to do with what is technologically possible, and everything to do with what the Neo-Victorians believe to be desirable and socially appropriate. The Neo-Victorians' schooling approaches seem at best, antiquated, and at

Box 7.2: *The Diamond Age*: Nanotechnology and disciplined children

> worst, punitive and oppressive. But as a story, is it believable? Can you imagine a future in which people might yearn to return to past educational traditions to quell anxieties about, and distaste for, the social and technological state of the present world?

Box 7.2 (*continued*)

It's probably inaccurate to suggest that the authors of *Ender's Game* and *The Diamond Age* genuinely think schools of the future will be as dull, didactic, and punitive as they portray them in their respective novels. More likely, these stereotypical representations of school have been deliberately chosen because they play on a conventional dramatic formula: A defiant child in a dull or oppressive schooling environment refuses to be disciplined by the system and instead embarks on their own life-learning journey—outside conventional school—which is what really enables them to become the heroes of their own stories.[15] It's these storylines that tell us what the authors think *really* powerful learning looks like and how it can best be enabled. In *The Diamond Age*, that protagonist is a young girl called Nell. You can see she is one of the girls copying texts in the Neo-Victorian classroom excerpt above, but that scene happens quite far into the book. Box 7.3 takes us back to a much earlier part in the book, and in Nell's life, where we'll find the beginnings of her own revolutionary learning journey outside the confines of school.

☙

---

15. This is roughly the storyline in classic English Bildungsromans (novels of development) such as *Jane Eyre* and *Oliver Twist* (except Oliver is in a workhouse rather than a school), along with Roald Dahl's *Matilda* (one teacher, Miss Honey, provides the nurturing learning that Matilda needs despite the abusive and hostile school environment created by the Headmistress, Miss Trunchbull), and many other children's and young adult books.

Subversive learning and the pursuit of "an interesting life"

Nell's story

Nell is a poor young girl from the disadvantaged underclass known as "thetes". In an early chapter of *The Diamond Age*, she accidentally comes into possession of a secret one-of-a-kind interactive tool with a very old-fashioned title: *The Young Lady's Illustrated Primer*, which has nothing whatsoever to do with the formal schooling system. Designed to pattern itself to its young reader, the *Primer* reacts to her environment and circumstances in order to develop an as-needed-when-needed personalised curriculum, in the form of a continuous story that helps her learn whatever she needs at that particular time. This is fantastic for Nell—it probably saves her life in fact—but where did the *Primer* come from? As it happens, it was the invention of Lord Alexander Finkle-McGraw, a high-ranking Neo-Victorian with a peculiar will to subvert the dominant educational paradigm of his own culture. His own educational philosophy is that education ought to lead the learner towards "an interesting life". As he says to another character in the book:

> in order to raise a generation of children who can reach their full potential, we must find a way to make their lives interesting. And the question I have for you, Mr Hackworth, is this: Do you think that our schools accomplish that? Or are they like the schools that Wordsworth complained of?

It is clear that Finkle-McGraw *doesn't* think the neo-Victorian schools support learners towards an interesting life, so he sets out to create something that will—the *Primer*—for his own young granddaughter, Elizabeth. The *Primer* was never intended for a young underclass child like Nell, but when an illicit duplicate copy falls mistakenly into her possession, it forever changes her own trajectory and that of a suite of other key characters and the wider social system.

Box 7.3: Subversive learning and the pursuit of "an interesting life"

The authors of *Ender's Game* and *The Diamond Age* seem to have chosen to tell rather depressing and conventional stories about future schools because, paradoxically, it enabled them to weave a story of a more desirable, exciting, personalised, transformative learning journey for Nell and Ender.[16] In both novels, the dramatic tension between these two stories about the purposes for education raise a number of deep and perhaps timeless debates. In both books, there are some adult characters whose main goal is to discipline, control, and standardise learners, and others whose goal is to empower learners to develop their own unique talents and use these to challenge or even subvert the status quo. Is the purpose of education to reproduce society, or to transform it? Should education be designed to help people live a more interesting or fulfilling life, or a life that adds value to society, or both? Where ought the balance lie? When all of us work together to imagine developing new learning environments and opportunities to give learners a better life, are we all thinking about all learners, or just those most familiar and similar to ourselves—or perhaps a talented, privileged few who seem to "deserve" something better? We aren't setting up these questions to give you answers. They don't have simple answers, but they are the kinds of questions we think need to be part of the wider conversation across society about future directions in education.

It is important that people don't just have these conversations in the abstract; we all need to have them as part of our collective work of

---

16. In both books, adults construct alternative learning environments specifically designed to nurture the young protagonists' talents and support them to develop their own deep capabilities through real, challenging (and sometimes even dangerous) experiences. These learning opportunities cultivate both Nell and Ender's potential to become people who can, and do, change the course of history. However, in Ender's case, the adults who manipulate him and his learning environment have a ruthlessly instrumental purpose: so that he may fulfil the destiny that The International Fleet has chosen for him (destroying the alien enemy), despite a great personal cost for Ender. The idea of powerful game-makers forcing people into real or simulated game arenas in order to manipulate them to their own ends is present in many other stories, including the recent *Hunger Games* book and film trilogy, the low-budget Canadian science-fiction film *Cube*, and of course the film *Gladiator*, all of which are underpinned by the historical reality that humans have indeed perpetrated these kinds of horrors on each other.

imagining and creating new ways to support future-building learning.[17] Whether you're a science-fiction writer or not, even your most imaginative future projections will contain some hard kernels of ideas that just make sense to you to retain and project into the future. The question is, how consciously or unconsciously do you gravitate towards certain theories, ideas, and assumptions, and how far are you willing to challenge or question these? As future-building educators, we all need to feel comfortable asking ourselves these questions, and helping others to do so.

Rigorous imagining and the future-building school
Let's leave science fiction and return to educationalist Keri Facer, who provides some advice for the prospective "future-building school". Such a school, she argues:

> takes seriously its responsibility to equip its students for the future [and] recognises that the old measures of future success … are no longer adequate to the task of driving a school's contribution to its students' and its community's future wellbeing. Instead, it takes on the more exciting, albeit more challenging, task of creating a meaningful debate with students and communities about the futures that are in development and the futures that they might want. It sets itself up as a partner for its students and its communities in generating visions of viable futures and as a resource to develop and build them.[18]

Facer suggests that schools and their communities need to undertake processes of "rigorous imagining", taking the seeds of different ideas about the future and pushing them further and further to see what they might lead to. As we've already seen, developing these ideas through stories, and populating them with believable characters, is one way that

---

17. For yet another argument for a greater public debate about the purposes of education, see this excerpt from British learning futurist David Price's book *Open: How We'll Live, Work, and Learn in the Future*. http://blogs.kqed.org/mindshift/2013/12/whats-our-vision-for-the-future-of-learning/
18. See Facer (2011), p. 107.

helps us imagine a more complete view of the future.[19] However we do it, Facer argues that it is important to be able to "emotionally occupy" the spaces of our imagined possible futures. She has a good point. All of us need to take the emotional dimensions of our futures thinking very seriously, because they play a big part of our default settings with regard to thinking about the future—whether these manifest as fear and anxiety, hopefulness and cheerful optimism, or even what futurist Richard Slaughter calls "the innate human tendency to prefer the known and to avoid the less well known".[20] Slaughter argues that this is happening on a vast scale today, and that "an inherent human conservatism suggests that we all want to continue with things as they are and in order to achieve this we'll sometimes actively tune out the signals that are informing us of very real dangers ahead".[21] He and other educational futurists are effectively calling on us to wake up, take a good hard look at the possible futures we are facing, shake off the urge to hide our heads in the sand, and get on with imagining and creating the future we want. Can we do it? We think so, otherwise we wouldn't have written this book. We also recognise that, as future-building educators, we'll need to actively cultivate our own resilience to get us through these

---

19. Facer (2011) models this approach in Chapter 8 of *Learning Futures* in which she imagines a school in the year 2035, described in narrative form through the eyes of a parent accompanying their daughter on her first day. See also the Q & A with Keri Facer (In press) in *set: Research Information for Teachers*. 1. In the same special issue, Hotere-Barnes, Bright, and Hutchings (In press) imagine a community-wide approach to schooling that supports te reo Māori revitalisation and support for whānau educational aspirations. See also Bolstad (2008) who imagines senior secondary learning in the year 2030 through the eyes of a student.
20. Slaughter (2010), p. 19.
21. Some research suggests our minds are subject to systematic inaccuracies in anticipating our own emotional responses to the future. Gilbert and Wilson (2009) explain how our brains generate mental simulations of future events (they use the analogy of a movie test screening), while another system in our brain views the simulation and produces an affective response (much like a test audience gives their feedback). The mind uses these simulations and responses to generate predictions about how we will feel when that event actually happens. The problem is, there are systematic errors both in the way the mental simulations are generated, and in the "test audience" responses. Dan Ariely's (2008) book *Predictably Irrational* provides further evidence of the ways in which our ability to make decisions about our futures, even in the short term, are inherently flawed but in somewhat predictable ways. All this makes us wonder how much better our thinking might be if we were more aware of, and able to work with, some of our intrinsic weaknesses as futures thinkers, rather than simply assuming that our big primate brains are well-suited to the demands of the task!

complex and challenging times. (And, as we've seen in earlier chapters, resilience is an important dimension of the key competency of *managing self*.) To inspire you further, in Box 7.4 we have one more story to tell you. This one isn't from science fiction. It's from real life, but it comes from another field: professional engineering.

Transition engineering

An analogy for future-building educators?

In early 2013 we met Professor Susan Krumdieck at a futures workshop. Susan is a transition engineer, based at the University of Canterbury. What is a transition engineer? As Susan explains, engineers like her who are concerned about sustainability have been chipping away for years to try to find different solutions for moving our current fossil-fuel dependent, carbon-emitting systems towards a more sustainable, less-destructive, post-carbon energy future. Yet we still haven't solved the problem of sustainable living. The emerging field of transition engineering is concerned with how we get from where we are now, to where environmental scientists and engineers believe we need to be in order to have continued social and environmental wellbeing far into the future. Where transition engineers think current approaches have fallen short is that we're facing a complex problem and trying to solve bits of the problem within too-narrow frames. For example, framing the future energy problem as primarily about our dependence on diminishing fossil fuels implies that alternative energies are the solution. Framing the problem as excess carbon emissions implies the solution is to reduce those emissions, or sequester more carbon. It's not that these solutions aren't useful, it's just that they aren't complete enough to get us out of our current problems. No narrow view of the problem will ever sufficiently address all its other dimensions.

Transition Engineering aims to provide a more holistic overall system for approaching this wicked problem. It is the work of delivering *change projects for existing systems* that reduce energy consumption resource use,

---

Box 7.4: Transition engineering

> waste production and environmental impacts while maintaining access to essential activities, goods and services. (Emphasis added.)
>
> Krumdieck argues that transition engineering can be viewed along the same lines as safety engineering. That branch of engineering emerged in the early 20th century as a response to workplace deaths. It ultimately led to changes in the professional ethics as well as the regulatory systems around professional engineering. Susan believes the starting point is for all engineering professionals to accept social responsibility for the long-term impacts of their professional work for people and the environment. In designing solutions for the built environment, transition engineers would see it as part of their professional responsibility to consider how their work now will impact on resource and energy use over a much longer period—potentially hundreds of years.
>
> Changing society's expectations of engineers is also part of the challenge. Engineers might take on transition engineering as part of their professional ethical responsibility. But if engineers' professional ethics are part of the supply-side solution, equivalent work is needed on the demand side. Society, and those who commission and develop the briefs for engineering projects, should *expect* engineers' work to support today's most sustainable approaches, and help us move towards the most sustainable system.

Box 7.4 (*continued*)

Your mission, should you choose to accept it …

Why did we choose transition engineering as the final example in this chapter? We think there are some interesting analogies between the scale and complexity of the change project that transition engineering is proposing, and the scale and complexity of the change project that we and others think is needed in education. What if we all took on the challenge to see ourselves as "transitional educators" (or, the term we've used in this chapter, "future-building educators")? What if we all saw our professional responsibility as being not only about supporting young people to plan for and create their futures, but supporting the whole system to move towards a new configuration that is more likely to build a better future for ourselves and our environment? What might we do differently in our day-to-day work, or over the scale of a week, year, or a phase of our lives or careers?

We hope that you come away with at least a few key messages from this chapter. For example, that the future is not predetermined. Any of us can project different possibilities and probabilities, but we can't know with any certainty what will happen. We think that seeing the future not just as something that will happen to us, but something that we collectively make happen, helps us take on a more empowered and active stance towards creating the future we want to see. In this chapter we have argued that, to create the future, we first need to be able not just to imagine, but to "rigorously imagine" and to keep pushing our ideas—with others—to see how far we can productively take them. At present, our education system is not necessarily geared towards these kinds of approaches—the knowledge-building, idea-improvement, "what if"? kinds of thinking that might help us all to become much more confident and capable future builders (although it is happening for some learners, for some of the time, in some schools, and we have put some of these stories in earlier chapters to give you inspiration).

As educational researchers, we have seen the power that lies in these kinds of approaches. We have talked to many school leaders, teachers, learners, families, other researchers, and community members who can see why these kinds of learning opportunities matter, how they positively impact on learners and other people. Above all, we have seen the productive energy and motivation that they can generate. We also know it is not easy.[22] As researchers, we know that research knowledge cannot act directly on the world; it is what people do with the research knowledge that matters. We hope our work contributes into this space by providing principles or ideas—supported by research and theory—that help people like you to do your own future-building work.

---

22. At NZCER for years we have talked about this kind of work as "hard fun".

8

Our take-home messages

So HERE WE ARE at the last few pages. We're glad you stuck with us, and there are just a few important things we'd like to recap before we end. Our hope is that the ideas about key competencies that we've explored will contribute to ongoing curriculum change. Whether and how that happens is up to all of us.

Opportunities for rigorous imagining can help us build a curriculum for the future

We all (educators, researchers, policy makers, students, parents, whānau, and other community members) have a part to play in making shifts happen across our education system. But first, we need collectively to develop some big-picture ideas about desirable futures—those most people could buy into. Unless we do that group development, change is unlikely to be more than tinkering around the edges of the system we have now. Once we know where we want to head, and why, plans for change are more likely to make sense and be seen as purposeful and worth investing in.

In this book we have used wicked problems as our own starting point to try and figure out the sorts of understandings and capabilities all young people will need if they are going to build a future for themselves, and for others, even in the face of difficult and complex changes in the world around them. We've modelled our own process of rigorous imagining, and also introduced the imaginings of a couple of science-fiction writers. We've used this imagining as a place to start exploring the kinds of learning experiences that could help us all create our preferred futures, for and with our young people.

Key competencies can be seen as a powerful metaphor for change
Throughout the book we've treated key competencies as an idea to think with, rather than as fixed entities. *NZC* made an important breakthrough by clearly signalling a need for shifts in curriculum thinking and planning, so that young people are supported to strengthen their capabilities for life now and in their futures. That's a great start, but we think there is scope to keep pushing the idea of capabilities so much further. We've shown how and where the *NZC* version of key competencies did—and did not—take up the ideas of the OECD. But we've also tried to move well beyond the OECD's still rather traditional change agenda to ask "what if" questions about ways key competencies could play a vital role at the centre of ongoing changes in our education system.

Imagining the capabilities that young people need
Right near the beginning of the book we introduced UNESCO's "four pillars for learning" in the 21st century. We noted that two of these pillars—"learning to be" and "learning to live with others"—are perhaps not such familiar targets for learning as "learning to know" and "learning to do". The futures-thinking process we've used has brought a number of ideas into view that might help us address uncertainties about learning to be and to live with others. As we've explained, we think that all students need opportunities to develop their capabilities, to be self-aware, critical, aware of interconnections, empathetic, creative, curious, and resilient.

Box 8.1 sets out our aspiration for young people. Just to be clear—we don't see these changes being made at the expense of developing deeper knowledge and understandings about the world. Quite the

> **Our aspiration is for young people who ...**
>
> ***Know who they are, what they value and why, and where they fit in.*** This self-awareness extends to recognising difference and appreciating that diversity is a resource to be treasured, not a problem to be managed away.
>
> ***Are willing and able to imagine what it might feel like to walk in others' shoes.*** They have a repertoire of skills and strategies for collaboration and for taking action to address issues that concern them and their communities.
>
> ***Question knowledge claims, rather than take them at face value.*** Since "right answers" do not come immediately to hand, these young people are willing to tolerate uncertainty, to keep thinking and exploring ideas and events in the pursuit of deeper understanding and a more fully developed view about how to tackle challenges they face.
>
> ***Look beyond immediate causes to consider the joined-up nature of things and events in the world.*** This sensitivity to interconnectedness leads to more thoughtfulness about the impact of personal and collective actions on others and environments—local and more distant—and ultimately on the planet as a whole. It is underpinned by ever-growing knowledge about how things work in the world.
>
> ***Think critically, creatively, and metacognitively****,* using a versatile repertoire of thinking types that they have developed and practised, and from which they can choose the most productive thinking approaches.
>
> ***Cultivate curiosity and a sense of wanting to know.*** They ask questions and pose problems to be solved, rather than only ever answering questions or addressing problems posed by others.
>
> ***Show resilience in the face of challenges and uncertainties.*** They accept that mistakes or dead ends are an important part of learning, especially when reaching for challenging goals. They know how and when to dust themselves off and try again.

Box 8.1: Our hopes for who young people can learn to be

opposite: deep knowledge is integral to the various ways of being we've just summarised, and as we have amply illustrated in the examples in previous chapters. But knowledge is not enough on its own. It's the rich mix of knowledge, skills, attitudes, and values—the specific capabilities that emerge in the various discipline areas—that give key competencies their power and their potential to educate the future builders our society will need. The emotional or dispositional components can't be neglected if these capabilities are to be useful and used, more immediately and in students' future lives.

Opportunities to learn

We know that teachers already "get" the powerful change potential in *NZC*. Some have found ways to factor students' possible futures into their thinking and ensure that learning matters for today and tomorrow. We see this in the way they are designing rich learning experiences that really stretch their students' current capabilities. Throughout the book we've included examples of what thoughtful and deliberate capability development can look like. We hope these examples will inspire other educators to try out capability-building ideas in their own contexts.

We'd also like to see these ideas pushed further. Just like the key competencies themselves, rich practice examples can also be ideas to think with, not just models to follow. With that sort of creative flexibility in mind, we end the book by briefly summarising our conclusions about the sorts of learning conditions that are more likely to foster capability development—and hence give expression to the key competencies in ways that contribute to future building. Looking across the stories from practice presented throughout this book, it is evident that there are certain learning opportunities that support key competency development. These include opportunities to:

- work on problems that are real to a group, class, community, or the world
- use established knowledge and the discourses associated with different types of knowledge in new ways and for new purposes
- work with diverse others, ideas, and values

- engage in collective knowledge building and collective action
- revisit ideas and actions over time—to think critically about, question, and alter, adapt, or improve on ideas or actions undertaken at any given point in time
- create links between opportunities to learn in different contexts.

Providing any one of the opportunities above tends to trigger the availability or presence of others. Our point here is that it doesn't really matter where you start so long as you have a big picture of where you want to go and some idea of how you might get there. Just jump in and go for it!

References

Apple, M. (2004). *Ideology and curriculum* (3rd ed.). New York and London: RoutledgeFalmer.

Apple, M., & Beane, J. (Eds.). (2007). *Democratic schools: Lessons in powerful education* (2nd ed.). Portsmouth, NH: Heinemann.

Ariely, D. (2008). *Predictably irrational*. New York: HarperCollins.

Barnett, R. (2004). Learning for an unknown future. *Higher Education Research and Development, 23*(3), 247–260.

Bereiter, C. (2002). *Education and mind in the knowledge age*. Mahwah, NJ: Erlbaum.

Bereiter, C., & Scardamalia, M. (2006). Education for the knowledge age: Design centered models of teaching and instruction. In P. Alexander & P. Winne (Eds.), *Handbook of educational psychology, second edition* (pp. 695–713). Mahwah, NJ: Erlbaum.

Bishop, P. (2005). *Framework forecasting: Managing uncertainty and influencing the future*. Paper presented at the Second Prague Workshop On Futures Studies Methodology Charles University, Czech Republic.

Bishop, P., & Hines, A. (2012). *Teaching about the future*. New York: Palgrave MacMillan.

Bolstad, R. (2008). A possible future? Senior secondary education in the year 2030. *set: Research Information for Teachers, 1*, 23–24.

Bolstad, R., Bull, A., Carson, C., Gilbert, J., MacIntyre, B., & Spiller, L. (2013). *Strengthening engagements between schools and the science community*. Wellington: Ministry of Education.

Bolstad, R., & Gilbert, J., with McDowall, S., Bull, A., Boyd, S., & Hipkins, R. (2012). *Supporting future-oriented learning and teaching: A New Zealand perspective*. Retrieved from http://www.educationcounts.govt.nz/publications/schooling/109306

Boyd, S. (2013). Student inquiry and curriculum integration: Ways of learning for the 21st century? (Part B). *set: Research Information for Teachers, 1*, 3–11.

Boyd, S., & Hipkins, R. (2012). Student inquiry and curriculum integration: Shared origins and points of difference. *set: Research Information for Teachers, 3*, 15–23.

Boyd, S., & Moss, M. (2009). *The changing face of Fruit in Schools: The 2008 case studies*. Final Healthy Futures evaluation report. Wellington: Ministry of Health.

Capra, F. (2002). *The hidden connections: Integrating the biological, cognitive, and social dimensions of life into a science of sustainability*. New York: Doubleday.

Card, O. S. (1992). *Ender's game*. London: Legend (original work published in 1985).
Dator, J. (In press). Four images of the future. *set: Research Information for Teachers, 1*.
Davis, B. (2004). *Inventions of teaching: A genealogy*. Mahwah, NJ: Earlbaum.
Davis, B., Sumara, D., & Luce-Kapler, R. (2000). *Engaging minds: Learning and teaching in a complex world*. Mahwah, NJ: Erlbaum.
Davis, B., Sumara, D., & Luce-Kapler, R. (2008). *Engaging minds: Changing teaching in complex times*. New York: Routledge.
Delandshere, G. (2002). Assessment as inquiry. *Teachers College Record, 104*(7), 1461–1484.
Delors, J. (1996). *Learning: The treasure within* (report to UNESCO by the International Commission on Education for the Twenty-First Century). Paris: UNESCO.
Delors, J. (Ed.). (1998). *Education for the twenty-first century*. Paris: UNESCO.
Dewey, J. (1916). *Democracy and education*. New York: Macmillan.
Draper, R., & Siebert, D. (2010). Re-thinking texts, literacies, and literacy across the curriculum. In R. Draper, P. Broomhead, A. Jensen, J. Nokes, & D. Siebert (Eds.), *(Re)imagining content-area literacy instruction* (pp. 20–39). New York: Teachers College Press.
Egan, K. (2008). *The future of schooling: Reimagining our schools from the ground up*. New Haven: Yale University Press.
Facer, K. (2011). *Learning futures: Education, technology and social change*. Abingdon, UK: Routledge.
Facer, K. (In press). Q&A. *set: Research Information for Teachers, 1*.
Frame, B., & Brown, J. (2008). Developing post-normal technologies for sustainability. *Ecological Economics, 65*(2), 225–241.
Fraser, D., Aitken, V., & Whyte, B. (2013). *Connecting curriculum, linking learning*. Wellington: NZCER Press.
Freire, P. (1993). *Pedagogy of the oppressed*. London: Penguin.
Gee, J. (2003). *What video games have to teach us about learning and literacy*. New York: Palgrave MacMillan.
Gee, J. (2007). *Sociolinguistics and literacies: Ideology in discourses* (3rd ed.). London: Routledge, Taylor and Francis Group.
Gibbons, A. (In press). 'Ah the serenity …' Absurd ideas about educational futures. *set: Research Information for Teachers, 1*.
Gilbert, D., & Wilson, T. (2009). Why the brain talks to itself: Sources of error in emotional prediction. *Philosphical Transactions of the Royal Society B, 364*, 1335–1341.
Gilbert, J. (2005). *Catching the knowledge wave? The knowledge society and the future of education*. Wellington: NZCER Press.
Harcourt, M., & Sheehan, M. (Eds.). (2012). *History matters: Teaching and learning history in New Zealand secondary schools in the 21st century*. Wellington: NZCER Press.
Hines, A., & Bishop, P. (Eds.). (2006). *Thinking about the future: Guidelines for strategic foresight*. Washington DC.: Social Technologies, LLC.
Hoskins, B. (2008). The discourse of social justice within European education policy developments: The example of key competences and indicator development towards

assuring the continuation of democracy. *European Educational Research Journal, 7*(3), 319–330.

Hotere-Barnes, A., Bright, N., & Hutchins, J. (In press). Reo and mātauranga Māori revitalisation: Learning visions for the future. *set: Research Information for Teachers, 1.*

Jackson, T. (2011). *Prosperity without growth: Economics for a finite planet.* London: Earthscan.

Johnson, L., & Morris, A. (2010). Towards a framework for critical citizenship education. *The Curriculum Journal, 21*(1), 77–96.

Kress, G. (2008). Meaning and learning in a world of instability and multiplicity. *Studies in Philosophy and Education, 27,* 253–266.

Lawrence, F. (2004). *Not on the label: What really goes into the food on your plate.* London: Penguin.

Leadbeater, C. (2011). *Rethinking innovation in education: Opening up the debate.* Melbourne: Centre for Strategic Innovation.

Lozano, J., Boni, A., Peris, J., & Hueso, A. (2012). Competencies in higher education: A critical analysis from the capabilities approach. *Journal of Philosophy of Education, 46*(1), 132–147.

Menand, L. (2002). *The metaphysical club.* London: Flamingo.

Michael, D., & Chen, S. (2005). *Serious games: Games that educate, train, and inform.* Muska & Lipman/Premier-Trade.

Ministry of Education. (2007). *The New Zealand curriculum.* Wellington: Learning Media.

Moje, E. (2008). Foregrounding the disciplines in secondary teaching and learning: A call for change. *Journal of Adolescent and Adult Literacy, 52*(2), 96–107.

Norris, S. (1997). Intellectual independence for nonscientists and other content-transcendent goals for science education. *Science Education, 81,* 239–258.

OECD. (2005). *The definition and selection of key competencies: Executive summary.* Retrieved from www.pisa.oecd.org/dataoecd/47/61/35070367.pdf

Office of the Prime Minister's Science Advisory Committee. (2013). *New Zealand's changing climate and oceans: The impact of human activity and implications for the future: An assessment of the current state of scientific knowledge by the Office of the Chief Science Advisor.* Wellington: Office of the Chief Science Advisor.

Ozeki, R. (1998). *My year of meats.* New York: Viking Press.

Perkins, D. (2009). *Making learning whole: How seven principles of teaching can transform education.* San Francisco: Jossey-Bass.

Pollan, M. (2006). *The omnivore's dilemma: A natural history of four square meals.* New York: Penguin.

Rayner, S. (2006). *Wicked problems: Clumsy solutions—diagnoses and prescriptions for environmental ills.* Jack Beale Memorial Lecture on Global Environment. Sydney: University of New South Wales.

Roberts, L., & Roberts, D. (2001). *Cinderella: An art deco love story.* London: Pavilion Children's Books.

Rutherford, J. (2005). Key competencies in the New Zealand curriculum development through consultation. *Curriculum Matters, 1,* 209–227.

Rychen, D., & Salganik, L. (Eds.). (2003). *Key competencies for a successful life and a well-functioning society*. Cambridge, MA: Hogrefe and Huber.
Shanahan, T., & Shanahan, C. (2012). What is disciplinary literacy and why does it matter? *Top Language Disorders, 32*(1), 7–18.
Slaughter, R. (2010). *The biggest wake-up call in history*. Indooroopilly, QA, Australia: Foresight International.
Sockett, H. (2012). *Knowledge and virtue in teaching and learning: The primacy of dispositions*. New York: Routledge.
Squire, K. (2006). From content to context: Videogames as designed experience. *Educational Researcher, 35*(8). 19–29.
Squire, K. (2011). *Video games and learning: Teaching and participatory culture in the digital age*. New York: Teachers College Press.
Stephenson, N. (1995). *The diamond age*. New York: Bantam Books.
Twist, J., & McDowall, S. (2010). *Life long literacy: The integration of key competencies and reading*. Wellington: New Zealand Council for Educational Research.
Walsh, P., (2013, February 8). Value of uni education extends beyond income. *NZ Herald* http://www.nzherald.co.nz/opinion/news/article.cfm?c_id=466&objectid=10864024
Washington, H., & Cook, J. (2011). *Climate change denial: heads in the sand*. London: Earthscan from Routledge.
Wright, P. (2013). Theory of knowledge or knowledge of the child? Challenging the epistemological assumptions of the curriculum debate on geography from an alternative viewpoint. *Oxford Review of Education, 39*(2), 193–210.

Index

acting autonomously, OECD key competency 13, 15, 16; compared to *NZC* key competency, managing self 14, 15
action-oriented approach to learning 98, 102
agency 28, 38, 98; individual and collective 111; to participate and contribute to collective actions 103–107
Aitken, Viv 87
Allan Wilson Centre 41, 42
American pragmatists 78
Anzac Day, example of teaching for diversity 40–41
Apple, Michael 57
aspirations for young people 135, 136, 137
assessment 16, 69; *see also* Programme for International Student Assessment (PISA)
Assessment Resource Bank (ARB) 58
authentic actions, in learning 27–28, 75

Barnett, Ronald 22
Bishop, Peter 119
Bull, Ally 64

capabilities: to contribute to society 99; for a decent life 99, 100, 114; to engage productively with wicked problems 24, 25, 98–99; imagining capabilities that young people need 135–137; key competencies as 16–18, 20, 21, 22, 69–71, 135, 137; meaning-making 90–93; needed to create social change and transformation within a group 103; related to self-awareness 21; science capabilities 88–90; subject-specific capabilities in using language, symbols and texts 88–90; for a successful life 98–99; for working with diverse others and ideas 34–36, 37–43, 44–46, 48–50, 119
Capra, Fritjof 60
change, understanding and influencing 119
cherry picking evidence 75, 77
choices: exploring different potential choices 71; food choices 54, 63, 67–68; understanding the consequences of personal choices 15, 54, 63, 68, 69, 70
Cinderella's father, example of teaching for diversity 38–39, 44, 45, 46, 47–48, 49
citizenship education 20, 100, 101, 112, 113–114
climate change 73–75, 96; strategies used to deny or explain away 76–77
"Climategate" 76
clumsy solutions 23; with diverse sets of values, knowledge and expertise 33

collective critical action 97–98, 99, 136, 138; connecting with learning areas 112–113; enabling students 101–107; and key competencies 107–111, 113–114
communities, creating and belonging to 109
competencies *see* capabilities; key competencies
complex problems: multiple dimensions 23, 62, 75, 113, 131–132; no one right answer 23, 61–62, 71, 75, 90, 110, 136
complex systems: social issues 90, 98; uncertainties 76, 77
complex systems thinking 27, 59–60, 71, 98
conspiracy theories 76
consumerism 96, 97
"contradictory certitudes" 23
creative thinking 61, 70, 91, 110–111
critical pedagogy 101
critical thinking 61, 70, 91, 136; about a decent life 110; about knowledge claims 75; in the food security context 66–67; revisiting ideas and actions 138; in taking critical and collective action 110
criticism, learning not to react negatively 62
cross-purposes, talking at 81–82
curiosity 10, 68, 91, 135, 136
curriculum: building for the future 134–135; choices 68–69; *see also New Zealand Curriculum (NZC)*

Dator, James 121
Davis, Brent 81
decent life: compared to successful life 98–99, 103, 128; enabling students to work collectively 101–107; and *New Zealand Curriculum (NZC)* 100–101, 113–114

Delors, Jaques 9
Delors Report 9, 11
deschooling 118
DeSeCo (Definition and Selection of Competencies) 12–14, 15, 120
Dewey, John 78, 101
The Diamond Age (Neal Stephenson) 125–126, 127, 128–129
disciplinary literacy 35, 46–47
disciplines 80; discipline-based meaning making 81, 82, 83–88, 89–90, 92–93, 137
discourses 34, 35–36, 81, 137; discipline-based compared to everyday 81, 88; public 83
dispositions: creating learning opportunities to address challenges 60–61, 62, 66–68, 91, 92; for creating social change and transformation within a group 103; people who know what to do in an unknown situation 22
diversity: capabilities needed for working with 34–36, 37–43, 44–46, 48–50, 119; and globalisation 33; learning opportunities 137; personal and emotional competencies required 45; teaching for 26, 37–50

economy: economic challenges, relative importance 98–99; economic instability 96, 97
Ecuador 65
education: citizenship education 101, 112, 113–114; environmental 103–105; as public good and private benefit 99; transformation of education systems for a better future 117–118
emergent properties of complex systems 60
emotions: competencies required for working with diversity 45; engaging, to shape learning experiences 68, 71;

and futures thinking 130; invoked in systems thinking 62
empathy, capacity for 36, 46, 70, 90–91
Ender's Game (Orson Scott Card) 122–124, 126, 128–129
engagement 27
enviro-club example of student agency in collective actions 103–105, 108, 109, 110–111, 112
Enviroschools trust 64–65
epistemic thinking 92
ethics: communities and groups 109–110; ethical thinking 91, 110
evaluation 69
evidence to support claims and ideas 38, 39, 41, 49, 66, 67, 71, 80–81; cherry picking 75, 77
expectations, impossible 76
experts: fake 76; trust in expert knowledge 74–75, 78–79

Facer, Keri 118, 129–130
fallacies, logical 76–77
fast food 56–57
Finland, Jokikunta Primary School 65
fishing and fish stocks 55–56, 57–58
food: ecological impacts of production 55–56, 57–58; food deserts 56–57; healthy eating 67–68; "rescue" services 63; in schools 55
food security 52–54; critical thinking 66–67; definitions 52; dilemmas 55–57; initiatives designed to help children understand 64–65; systems thinking 57–58, 60–68
food web, in a home garden 58–59
frameworks: *New Zealand Curriculum* 8–9, 10, 29; *Te Marautanga o Aotearoa* 29
future forecasting 119, 120
future, in science fiction 120–129
future-building educators: future building not future proofing 118–119; and the future-building school 129–132; future-focused thinking 28, 29–31, 37–38; key competencies for 119–120; rethinking the future of learning 116–117, 128–129; rigorous imagining and building a curriculum for the future 134–135; transformation of education systems for a better future 117–118, 132–133; transition engineering: an analogy 131–132
future-focused thinking 18, 19; attributes of people who know what to do in an unknown situation 22; complex systems 27; future of learning 116–117; *NZC* key competencies 20–22, 29–31, 116; *see also* wicked problems

games, educational 124
garden food web 58–59
Garden to Table trust 64
Gee, James 34, 35
Gilbert, Jane 19, 37, 38
globalisation 20, 33, 100
"group think" 110
groups: ensuring group diversity 49; individual identity within 110; *NZC* key competencies relating to 10, 14, 15–16; OECD key competency 13, 14, 15–16; opportunities for students to work with others 49, 98, 101–107, 108; opportunities for using group diversity to learn 47–48; *see also* collective critical action

Health and Physical Education learning area 108, 112
health promotion 108
"healthy chocolate" meaning-making example 84–85
Healthy Communities and Environments Strand 112
healthy eating 67–68

historical thinking 81, 86

identities: and managing self 36; taking on, within a discourse community 35
imagination 61
income disparities 33, 95–96, 98
individual and competitive approaches to learning 98, 101
inequalities 95–96, 98
inquiry cycle, student 102
interconnections 65–68, 70, 135, 136
International Commission on Education for the Twenty-first Century 9; *Learning: The Treasure Within* (Delors Report) 9, 11
"it depends" thinking 58–60, 61–62, 70

Jackson, Tim 97
Jokikunta Primary School, Finland 65
jurisprudence 78

Kaibosh, "food rescue" service 63
Kaimanawa horse culling, meaning-making example 87–88
key competencies: OECD four competencies 13, 14–16, 98–99, 135; origin of the idea 9, 11–14; as a powerful metaphor for change 135; social-justice narrative 99; and a well-functioning society 98–99
Key Competencies and Effective Pedagogy project 39
key competencies in *New Zealand Curriculum* 5–6, 10, 14–16; as capabilities 16–18, 20, 21, 22, 69–71, 135, 137; comparison of OECD and *NZC* key competencies 14–16; future focus 20–22, 29–31, 116; for future-building educators 119–120; market-driven 99; supporting systems thinking 60–63; in taking critical and collective action 107–111, 113–114; teaching for competency development 68–69, 70–71; *see also* specific competencies, e.g. managing self
knowledge: accessing established knowledge to solve shared problem 48; assumption that knowledge is true and stable 74–75; collective knowledge building 138; community advancement of 38; knowledge needed for working with diverse others and ideas 46–47; knowledge-building conventions 80–81, 82, 83; knowledge-centred curriculum 38; providing opportunities for collective knowledge building 49; public knowledge 79, 80–83, 91; supporting students to build 48–49, 135, 137; using in new ways 137; views about 29, 30, 37
knowledge claims: contested 71, 73, 74–75, 77–79, 92–93, 136; evidence bases for 38, 39, 41, 49, 66, 67, 71, 80–81; learning when to trust experts 77–79; public knowledge-claims 79, 80–83; strategies used to deny or explain away 75–77; taking at face value 91–92; *see also* meaning-making
Krumdieck, Susan 131–132

language learning 21
Leadbeater, Charles 30
learning: addressing dispositional challenges 62, 66–68, 91, 92; in different contexts 138; future of 116–117, 128–129; individual and competitive approaches 98, 101; "learning about" 98, 102; learning by doing 98, 101, 102; learning opportunities 137–138; limitations on student opportunities 37; using group diversity 47–48; "whole learning" 75; *see also* meaning-making

learning areas 9, 10, 37; and collective critical action 112–113; Health and Physical Education 108, 112; Learning Languages 21; Science 81
learning, Delors Report "pillars": to be 9, 11, 135; to do 9, 11, 135; to know 9, 11, 135; to live together 9, 11, 135
Learning: The Treasure Within (Delors Report) 9, 11
LENS science outreach programme 66, 67–68
"library of experiences" 64–65
Life Long Literacy project 38, 61–62
Liggins Institute, LENS science outreach programme 66, 67–68
literate practice, in disciplines and subject areas 35
logical fallacies 76–77

making a difference by working together *see* collective critical action
malnutrition 56–57
managing self, *NZC* key competency 10, 14, 15, 36, 131; associated capabilities 70, 91, 92; capabilities needed for working with diversity 45; compared to OECD key competency, acting autonomously 14, 15; skills needed to debate ideas 39; in systems thinking 62
"Mantle of the Expert" 87
Māori: food security 55; socioeconomic data 66
mātauranga Māori 42, 44, 47
meaning-making 73–75, 79–81; as classroom focus 83–88; conventions 80–81, 82, 83, 89–90; discipline-based 81, 82, 83–88, 89–90, 92–93, 137; opportunities to develop capabilities 90–93; *see also* knowledge claims; learning media: learning how "truth" is established 85–86; role in a

democracy 86; role in shaping public opinion 78–79
mental models 37, 74
minds, as containers 37
misrepresentations 76–77
"mob mentality" 110–111
Moje, Elizabeth 46–47
Monckton, Lord 76

New Zealand Curriculum (NZC): "back half" 21; "front half" 21; overall structure 8–9, 10; principles 10, 20, 100; space to focus on a decent life 100–101; values 10; vision 10, 11, 20, 100; *see also* key competencies in *New Zealand Curriculum;* learning areas
Norris, Stephen 78

Organisation for Economic Co-operation and Development (OECD) 11–14; four key competencies 13, 14–16, 98–99, 135; report on income gaps 95–96

participating and contributing, *NZC* key competency 10, 14, 36; associated capabilities 70, 92; capabilities needed for working with diversity 45–46, 49; compared to OECD key competency relating to groups 14, 15–16; in systems thinking 63; in taking critical and collective action 107, 109, 114
Pasifika people: food security 55; socioeconomic data 66
peers, working with 108
Perkins, David 75, 79
Philosophical Chairs model 40, 45–46, 50
poverty 22, 55, 95, 96
praxis 101
Price, David 129
Programme for International Student Assessment (PISA) 11–12

public knowledge 79, 91;
  characteristics 80–83

reading: agency and authority 38–39;
  managing self, relating to others, and
  participating and contributing 45, 46;
  use of language, symbols and texts, and
  thinking 44
relating to others, *NZC* key
  competency 10, 14, 36; associated
  capabilities 70, 91; capabilities needed
  for working with diversity 45–46, 49;
  in systems thinking 62–63; in taking
  critical and collective action 108
resilience 22, 62, 130–131, 135, 136
"rigorous imagining" 129–130, 133,
  134–135
Robinson, Sir Ken 117
Rutherford, Justine 15

school food 55
schools, future-building 129–132
schools, representations in science
  fiction: *The Diamond Age* (Neal
  Stephenson) 125–126, 127,
  128–129; *Ender's Game* (Orson Scott
  Card) 122–124, 126, 128–129
science 21–2; "healthy chocolate"
  meaning-making example 84–85;
  learning area 81; learning to make
  meaning of scientists' texts 83–84;
  Nature of Science strand 81, 88, 89;
  science capabilities 88–90; science
  wānanga 42–43, 44, 47; theory 81
science fiction 120–129
Seixas, Peter 81
self-management *see* managing self, *NZC*
  key competency
Slaughter, Richard 130
social justice 99, 110
social meaning-making conventions 82
society, and competency development 90,
  98–99

Sockett, Hugh 79
Steiner philosophy of schooling 61
successful life 98–99, 103, 128
sustainability 11, 20, 42, 43, 47, 56, 63,
  64, 65, 97, 100, 110, 112, 131–132
systems thinking 27, 54, 91; complex
  systems 27, 59–60, 71, 76, 98; how
  key competencies support 60–63; as a
  specific dimension of thinking 57–60;
  teaching that develops 64–68

Te Marautanga o Aotearoa 29
technological change, and access to diverse
  others around the world 33
thinking: about interconnections 65–68,
  70, 135, 136; creative thinking 61,
  70, 91, 110–111, 136; epistemic
  thinking 92; ethical thinking 91, 110;
  for future-building educators 120;
  historical thinking 81, 86; "it depends"
  thinking 58–60, 61–62, 70; and
  meaning-making 79, 82, 90; OECD
  key competency 13, 14–15, 17; *see
  also* critical thinking; future-focused
  thinking; systems thinking
thinking, *NZC* key competency 10,
  14, 15, 35, 57, 79; associated
  capabilities 70; capabilities needed for
  working with diversity 44
tools, using interactively: *NZC* key
  competencies relating to 10, 14;
  OECD key competency 13
transition engineering: analogy for future-
  building educators 131–132
Treaty of Waitangi 11

Uawanui, example of teaching for
  diversity 41–43, 44, 45, 46, 47, 48
uncertainties: complex systems 23, 76, 77;
  learning to manage 39, 69, 70, 136;
  public-knowledge claims 79, 136; in
  systems thinking 62

United Nations Educational, Scientific and Cultural Organization (UNESCO) 9; "four pillars for learning" 9, 11, 135; International Commission for Education for the Twenty-first Century 120

University of Otago 41, 42, 43

using language, symbols and texts, *NZC* key competency 10, 14, 34–35, 66; capabilities needed for working with diversity 44; and meaning-making 79, 82, 90; subject-specific capabilities 88–90

values: clarification of 91; communities and groups 109–110; and food security 61, 63; *New Zealand Curriculum* 10; personal 11, 47, 70, 71, 77, 136; and working on solutions to wicked problems 33, 50, 75

virtual mobility 33

Waitangi Day, example of teaching for diversity 39–40, 45–46, 48

Walsh, Pat 99

war memorialisation, example of teaching for diversity 40–41, 44, 48, 49

"whole learning" 75

whole, more than the sum of the parts 26–27

wicked problems 19, 22–24, 31, 113, 116; attributes of people who know what to do in an unknown situation 22; energy future 131–132; multiple dimensions 23, 62, 75, 113, 131–132; no one right answer 23, 61–62, 71, 75, 90, 110, 136; transformation of education systems for a better future 117–118; as a useful conceptual tool for educators 24–25; *see also* climate change; clumsy solutions; food security; globalisation; inequalities

Woodham, Carly 56
world views 33, 44, 98
World Wildlife Fund (WWF) 56
Wright, Philip 61

Youth Health Council example of student agency in collective actions 105–107, 108, 109, 110, 111, 112

www.ingramcontent.com/pod-product-compliance
Lightning Source LLC
Chambersburg PA
CBHW050123020526
44112CB00035B/2372